Michelle Obama

Other books in the People in the News series:

Michelle Obama

by Michael V. Uschan

LUCENT BOOKS

An imprint of Thomson Gale, a part of The Thomson Corporation

GALE
CENGAGE Learning™

Acknowledgement
The author would like to dedicate this book to Dr. Durelle Chopp, another strong woman who has made a difference in the lives of thousands of students as an educator.

© 2010 Gale, Cengage Learning

LIBRARY OF CONGRESS CATALOGING-IN-PUBLICATION DATA

Uschan, Michael V., 1948-
  Michelle Obama / by Michael V. Uschan.
    p. cm. -- (People in the news)
  Includes bibliographical references and index.
  ISBN 978-1-4205-0209-1 (hardcover)
  1. Obama, Michelle, 1964---Juvenile literature. 2. Presidents' spouses--United States--Bi-ography--Juvenile literature. 3. Legislators' spouses--United States--Biography--Juvenile literature. 4. African American women lawyers--Illinois--Chicago--Biography--Juvenile literature. 5. Chicago (Ill.)--Biography--Juvenile literature. 6. African American women--Biography--Juvenile literature. I. Title.

  E909.O24U83 2010
  973.932092--dc22
  [B]
                                                            2009036557

Lucent Books
27500 Drake Rd.
Farmington Hills, MI 48331

ISBN-13: 978-1-4205-0209-1
ISBN-10: 1-4205-0209-3

Printed in the United States of America
1 2 3 4 5 6 7 13 12 11 10 09

Printed by Bang Printing, Brainerd, MN, 1ˢᵗ Ptg., 12/2009

Contents

Fame and celebrity are alluring. People are drawn to those who walk in fame's spotlight, whether they are known for great accomplishments or for notorious deeds. The lives of the famous pique public interest and attract attention, perhaps because their experiences seem in some ways so different from, yet in other ways so similar to, our own.

Newspapers, magazines, and television regularly capitalize on this fascination with celebrity by running profiles of famous people. For example, television programs such as *Entertainment Tonight* devote all their programming to stories about entertainment and entertainers. Magazines such as *People* fill their pages with stories of the private lives of famous people. Even newspapers, newsmagazines, and television news frequently delve into the lives of well-known personalities. Despite the number of articles and programs, few provide more than a superficial glimpse at their subjects.

Lucent's People in the News series offers young readers a deeper look into the lives of today's newsmakers, the influences that have shaped them, and the impact they have had in their fields of endeavor and on other people's lives. The subjects of the series hail from many disciplines and walks of life. They include authors, musicians, athletes, political leaders, entertainers, entrepreneurs, and others who have made a mark on modern life and who, in many cases, will continue to do so for years to come.

These biographies are more than factual chronicles. Each book emphasizes the contributions, accomplishments, or deeds that have brought fame or notoriety to the individual and shows how that person has influenced modern life. Authors portray their subjects in a realistic, unsentimental light. For example, Bill Gates —the cofounder and chief executive officer of the software giant Microsoft—has been instrumental in making personal computers the most vital tool of the modern age. Few dispute his business savvy, his perseverance, or his technical expertise, yet critics say he is ruthless in his dealings with competitors and driven more by his desire to maintain Microsoft's dominance in the computer industry than by an interest in furthering technology.

In these books, young readers will encounter inspiring stories about real people who achieved success despite enormous obstacles. Oprah Winfrey—the most powerful, most watched, and wealthiest woman on television today—spent the first six years of her life in the care of her grandparents while her unwed mother sought work and a better life elsewhere. Her adolescence was colored by promiscuity, pregnancy at age fourteen, rape, and sexual abuse.

Each author documents and supports his or her work with an array of primary and secondary source quotations taken from diaries, letters, speeches, and interviews. All quotes are footnoted to show readers exactly how and where biographers derive their information and provide guidance for further research. The quotations enliven the text by giving readers eyewitness views of the life and accomplishments of each person covered in the People in the News series.

In addition, each book in the series includes photographs, annotated bibliographies, timelines, and comprehensive indexes. For both the casual reader and the student researcher, the People in the News series offers insight into the lives of today's newsmakers—people who shape the way we live, work, and play in the modern age.

A First Lady Like No Other

On February 18, 2009, Michelle Obama turned the East Wing of the White House into a classroom by hosting a celebration of Black History Month. In an informal lecture to nearly two hundred sixth- and seventh-grade students from Washington, D.C., schools, Obama detailed the role the White House has played in African American history. She told students that from 1793 to 1800 black slaves helped build the huge, ornate building that is the president's home and office. Obama also explained that in 1863 President Abraham Lincoln signed the Emancipation Proclamation in a White House room that was later named after him. She also told students that in the 1960s, President John F. Kennedy and President Lyndon B. Johnson each met with Dr. Martin Luther King Jr. and other black leaders in the White House to help blacks gain the civil rights that many Southern states were still denying them.

When the students told Obama they already knew those facts, she was delighted. "So you guys know your history. That's a good thing," she said. "That means your parents and teachers are doing their jobs."[1] Obama then asked the youths if they knew why her husband, Barack Obama, was also making history. When many students tried to respond to her question, Obama asked a girl who was yelling louder than anyone else to give the answer. The student rose to her feet and explained that "he's the first African

Michelle Obama hugs a student who attended a celebration of Black History Month, hosted by the First Lady, at the White House on February 18, 2009.

American president of the United States of America."[2]

What Michelle Obama did not ask was if the students knew that she was making history, too, as the nation's first African American First Lady.

A Milestone in African American History

Barack Obama's inauguration as the first African American U.S. president on January 20, 2009, shattered a racial barrier that many people believed might never be broken because of racism.

His election was seen as an important symbolic step forward for African Americans, who for most of the last five centuries have been treated unfairly and sometimes brutally by whites in the United States.

In 1609 the first African Americans arrived in the land that would become the United States. A ship brought them from Africa to Virginia, then a British colony, and they were sold as slaves. When colonists won their freedom in 1783 from Great Britain and created the United States, the new nation allowed slavery to continue even though the Declaration of Independence, written in 1776, states that "all men are created equal."[3] Although the government ended slavery in 1865, many African Americans were denied basic rights and discriminated against because of the color of their skin for another century. Blacks in many states during that period were not allowed to vote, live in areas reserved for whites, or use restrooms, restaurants, hotels, and other public places that were reserved for whites.

Barack Obama's ancestors never suffered such cruel treatment—his father was an immigrant from Kenya and his mother was white—but Michelle Obama's did. In 1850 James Robinson, Michelle's great-great-grandfather, was born a slave in South Carolina. Her family lived in segregated South Carolina until her grandfather, Fraser Robinson Jr., moved to Chicago, Illinois, in the early 1930s. In South Carolina, her ancestors were denied basic rights, like voting, and were forced to live under segregation. Illinois and other northern states allowed blacks more freedom than southern states, but members of her family were still discriminated against in where they could live and in hiring practices for jobs.

A Unique First Lady

Michelle Obama's slave ancestry is the most dramatic aspect of her family history. U.S. representative James E. Clyburn, a South Carolina Democrat, claims that having a descendant of slaves as First Lady is as meaningful historically as her husband's status as the first black president. Clyburn has even predicted that

Obama's ancestry can help erase the stigma of the nation's slave past: "I believe she could play as pivotal a role as her husband could, if not more so. It would allow us an opportunity to get beyond some of our preconceived notions, some of our prejudices."[4] Although some African Americans have trouble accepting the slave pasts in their own history, Obama has embraced it as an example of how blacks and whites have a shared history. She says,

> An important message in this journey is that we're all linked [through] our histories of growth and survival in this country. Somewhere there was a slave owner—or a white family in my great-grandfather's time that [after slavery ended] gave him a place, a home, that helped him build a life—that again led to me. So who were those people? I would argue they're just as much a part of my history as my great-great-grandfather.[5]

A slave cabin where it is believed that Michelle Obama's great-great-grandfather James lived. Being a descendent of slaves makes Obama an historic First Lady.

The color of her skin and family history make Obama a First Lady like no other in the nation's history. Her job history also made her unique among First Ladies. Obama is an attorney and continued working even after having two daughters. In fact, she did not quit her last job, vice president for the University of Chicago Medical Center, until her husband was elected president. Obama's race and history of hard work have also made her a role model for African Americans and all working mothers.

An Inspiration

During her husband's campaign for president, Obama visited many states to help him win the election. At many of her appearances, blacks told her that she and her husband had already inspired them by enabling them to think they could do great things, too, despite the color of their skin. In a beauty parlor in South Carolina, Obama met a ten-year-old girl who told her that if Barack won the election, then "it means I can imagine anything for myself."[6] The little girl then began crying with happiness at that thought.

During a campaign speech for her husband at the annual luncheon for the National Partnership for Women and Families in June 2008, Michelle talked about the challenges of being a working mother.

Obama is also admired by working mothers of all races who face the same problems she does in trying to care for her children and hold down a job. In many speeches to women during the campaign, Obama explained how hard she had struggled to be both a mother and career woman and anguished over whether she was doing a good job at both those difficult tasks. Letitia Baldrige is an author who was First Lady Jacqueline Kennedy's social secretary and chief of staff from 1960 to 1963. Baldrige believes Obama will continue to impress women as First Lady, because she will have to juggle the many duties of that position while still raising her two children. Baldrige says, "That's where she can inspire women of today, who are frantically trying to work their way up in the world and be compensated properly. Michelle is always going back to her kids. She will help women realize that a woman can juggle the two, that she can find that division between family and job, and experience joy in both places."[7]

Chapter 1

Growing Up in Chicago

In 2007 when Barack Obama began running for president, he spent time during each campaign appearance telling his life story so voters could get to know him. Michelle Obama did the same thing. In city after city around the country, she talked with pride about her past, especially about the wonderful way her parents had raised her. In January 2008 Obama told a large audience in New Hampshire that "deep down inside I'm still that little girl who grew up on the South Side of Chicago. Everything that I think about and do is shaped around the life I lived in that bungalow that my father worked so hard to provide for us."[8]

Obama always mentioned that her parents both played an important role in creating the woman she became. She has said pointedly that "my lens of life, how I see the world, is through my background, my upbringing."[9]

Fraser and Marian Robinson

Michelle LaVaughn Robinson was born in Chicago, Illinois, on January 17, 1964. Her parents were Fraser Robinson III, a city water plant employee, and Marian Shields Robinson, a traditional mom who stayed home to raise her children. Obama's brother, Craig, is eighteen months older than she is, but they were so close in age and looked so much alike that people often thought they were twins. Obama said her parents created a tight-knit, loving

Michelle and her brother had traditional childhoods, with their mother, Marian Robinson, staying at home to raise them.

family atmosphere that made her feel protected "[My dad] and my mom poured everything they had into me and Craig. It was the greatest gift a child could receive, never doubting for a single minute that you were loved and cherished and have a place in this world."[10]

The family rented the upper flat of a small, two-story home in Chicago's South Shore area from a great-aunt, who lived on the first floor and taught piano. The flat had so little space that Fraser built a partition in the living room so Michelle and Craig could have their own bedrooms. Chicago in the 1960s was one of the nation's most segregated cities and the South Shore—it got its name from its proximity to Lake Michigan—was one area in which blacks had always lived. Although some sections of South Shore were troubled by gangs in the 1960s, the Robinsons lived near the University of Chicago Hospitals in a better neighborhood that included some whites.

Obama idolized her dad while she was growing up. In addition

Black History and Michelle Obama

Michelle Obama's family history closely parallels the history of other African American families. In 1619 the first twenty African Americans arrived as slaves in the British colony of Virginia. By the end of the Civil War in 1865 there were more than four million African Americans in America, most living as slaves. Jim Robinson, Obama's great-great-grandfather, was born a slave in 1850 on Fairfield Plantation in Georgetown, South Carolina. Even after slaves were free, southern states denied Robinson and his descendants their basic rights, like being able to vote, for another century.

In the early 1930s Fraser Robinson Jr., Obama's grandfather, moved to Chicago, Illinois. He was one of millions of blacks who moved to northern states to escape racism in the South during the first half of the twentieth century. In Chicago he married LaVaughn Johnson and worked for the U.S. Postal Service. Racism was less overt in northern states, but even in the 1960s, Chicago blacks went to segregated schools, lived in segregated communities, and faced job discrimination. During the 1960s, civil rights leaders like Martin Luther King Jr. gave Southern blacks equality with whites by overturning racist laws that denied blacks many basic rights. In the summer of 1966, two years after Obama was born, King protested segregated housing and education in Chicago. Violence erupted during marches he led into white areas, which showed that racism was still strong when Obama was a little girl.

to being a loving father, Fraser was also a hero to her because he continued working despite being handicapped by multiple sclerosis, a disease that slowly degenerates muscle control. In his youth Fraser had been a fine athlete who boxed and swam, but the disease began robbing him of his mobility as an adult. At first he walked with a limp, but gradually he had more trouble getting around, which forced him at times to use a cane, crutches, and even a motorized wheelchair. Obama admired her father because despite the illness, he kept working at the water plant and never complained about his medical problem. Obama said,

> My dad was our rock. And although he was diagnosed with multiple sclerosis in his early 30s, he was our provider. He was our champion, our hero. [If] he was in pain, he never let on. He never stopped smiling and laughing, even while struggling to button his shirt, even while using two canes to get himself across the room to give my mom a kiss. He just woke up a little earlier and he worked a little harder.[11]

Robinson also expected his children to work hard and live up to his high standards of behavior. When they failed to do that, he would not raise his voice or beat them. Instead, Robinson would stare coldly at his children and tell them how much they had disappointed him. Michelle and Craig loved and respected their dad so much that they felt bad when he did that. Obama said they would even start crying because "you never wanted to disappoint him. We would be bawling."[12]

Luckily for Obama, she rarely made her dad cry. She was a well-behaved child who rarely caused her parents any worry.

Obama's Childhood

When Michelle was little, she did things most young girls do. She had an EASY-BAKE Oven and she had a dollhouse and African American Barbie and Ken dolls. Unlike most little girls, however, Michelle began learning to read when she was only four years old. She wanted to learn, because she was jealous that Craig was already reading. Once she took one of his books and told her mother she was going to teach herself to read. When Michelle failed at that impossible task, her mom taught her how to read.

According to Marian Robinson, Michelle was an intelligent, independent little girl who was not afraid to try new things and who managed her own life even at young age. Robinson said, "I always say Michelle raised herself from about nine years old. She had her head on straight very early."[13] One aspect of that adult approach to life was her dedication to learning to play the

Michelle and Her Dad Register Voters

Democrats have ruled Chicago politics since the early twentieth century. They have succeeded in this by making sure that all Democrats are registered to vote and that they vote on Election Day. The Democratic Party depends on people at the precinct level—a precinct is one voting area in the city—to do this work. Obama's dad, Fraser Robinson III, was a Democratic Party precinct captain who helped register voters. Even though Robinson did not trust some local politicians, he did that because he believed the party did a lot to help poor and working class people. Obama says,

> Some of my earliest memories are of tagging along with him as we'd walk door to door and help folks register to vote. We'd sit in neighbors' kitchens for hours and listen to their opinions, their concerns, and the dreams they had for their children. And before we left those kitchens, my father would make sure that everyone could get to the voting booth on Election Day—because he knew that a single vote could help make their dreams a reality.

Quoted in David Colbert, "*Michelle Obama: An American Story*", New York: Houghton Mifflin Harcourt, 2009, pp. 10–11.

piano. Her great-aunt taught Michelle how to play. Robinson said Michelle "would practice the piano for so long you'd have to tell her to stop."[14]

The Robinsons lived a quiet, family-oriented life. They ate their meals together and often played board games, like Chinese Checkers and Monopoly. According to her brother, Michelle hated to lose so much that when they played games, he would sometimes let her win so she would not quit. Craig says, "My sister is a poor sport. She didn't like to lose."[15] The Robinson children had a lot of time for games and for reading because their parents only allowed them to watch one hour of television each day.

As the children grew older, some of their free time was spent doing household chores. Every Saturday, Michelle had to thoroughly clean the bathroom, from mopping the floor to scrubbing the toilet. The siblings also alternated washing dishes, with Michelle doing them Tuesday, Thursday, and Saturday nights. During summer vacations, the family took trips to Dukes Happy Holiday Resort in Michigan or to visit grandparents and other relatives in South Carolina.

As a young girl, Michelle liked fashionable clothes and accessories. She was able to indulge that passion after she began earning money babysitting. But when Michelle came home one day with a bag by Coach, her mother was upset she had spent so much money for a designer purse. Michelle defended her purchase, claiming the bag was so versatile she could use it for any occasion and would not have to buy several other purses. Robinson said that was one of the few times she ever had to criticize her daughter. "If she ever did do anything naughty, she was smart enough not to let me find out about it,"[16] said Robinson.

A Good Student

Both of Michelle's parents believed a good education would help their children be successful even though neither parent had attended college. They prodded Craig and Michelle to study hard and even persuaded school officials to let them skip second grade. They felt Michelle and Craig already knew so much that they

Because her brother, Craig, was such a gifted student, Michelle had to work much harder to get the same grades that he brought home.

needed to advance to a higher grade to be challenged. After skipping the second grade, both children continued to rank among the brightest students in their classes.

Michelle, however, discovered it was not easy following Craig through the local school system. The problem was that Craig was such a gifted student that teachers automatically expected the same sort of excellence from her. Michelle tried to keep up with her brother, but it was not as easy for her to get top grades as it had been for Craig. Robinson admits,

> She was disappointed in herself. She used to have a little bit of trouble with tests, so she did whatever she had to, to

make up for that. I'm sure it was psychological because she was hard working and she had a brother who could pass a test just by carrying a book under his arm. When you are around someone like that, even if you are OK, you want to be as good or better.[17]

Thus Michelle had to work harder to get the same grades her brother brought home so easily. Michelle worked so hard that she even impressed Craig, who said, "I'd come home from basketball practice, and she'd be working. I'd sit down on the couch and watch TV; she'd keep working. When I turned off the TV, she'd still be working."[18]

The hard work enabled Michelle to excel in school. By the time she was in sixth grade, she was in the gifted class at Bryn Mawr Elementary School, which today is known as Bouchet Math and Science Academy. In the gifted class, Michelle studied French for three years and took advanced biology classes at Kennedy-King College. Biology classmate Chiaka Davis Patterson said Michelle did lab work that included identifying the muscles of rats that had been dissected. "This is not what normal seventh-graders were getting,"[19] Patterson said. Michelle performed so well that she finished second in her Bryn Mawr graduating class of a hundred students.

Michelle now had to decide which high school to attend. Although a neighborhood public school was only a block away from the Robinson home, Craig had enrolled in Mount Carmel, a private boys' school with tough academic standards and an outstanding sports program. The latter was important for Craig, a talented 6-foot, 5-inch (1.8m, 12.7cm) basketball player, who would become good enough to win an athletic scholarship to college. Michelle also decided to bypass the neighborhood school and attend Whitney M. Young, Chicago's first magnet high school. She chose Whitney M. Young even though the school was so far away that she had to leave home at 6 A.M. daily to make the ninety-minute trip by bus and elevated train. Michelle accepted the three-hour round-trip commute because she knew the school's strong academic program would give her the best education possible.

Life at Whitney M. Young

Like many other big cities, Chicago in the 1970s was trying to integrate its schools. To lure white and black students away from schools in their segregated neighborhoods, the Chicago district began opening magnet schools. Although Whitney M. Young was an integrated school, it still had more black students than white students. Among the students were the children of the city's most influential African Americans, including Santita Jackson, the daughter of Baptist minister and civil rights activist Jesse Jackson.

Going to Whitney M. Young separated Obama not only geographically from her old neighborhood but also culturally because many of her fellow students' families were better off financially than hers was. Like her, most of Whitney M. Young's students believed it was important to get a good education. But in her neighborhood and other parts of Chicago, Obama sometimes met young blacks who hated school and sometimes mocked fellow blacks who studied hard and were good students. Obama began trying to hide her schooling so she would not be picked on. She called this social tactic "speaking two languages." Obama explains, "What I learned growing up is that if I'm not going to get my butt kicked every day after school, I can't flaunt my intel-

During her high school years, Michelle attended an integrated school like the one pictured here.

ligence in front of peers who are struggling with a whole range of things. [You have] to be smart without acting smart."[20]

Obama began high school in 1977, two years after Whitney M. Young opened. English teacher Dagny Bloland says in that period in Chicago "the tradition of leaving one's neighborhood to go to high school was very new, and a person had to be very gutsy to do

The Importance of Education

Education was very important in the Robinson family and Michelle Obama has degrees from Princeton University and Harvard Law School. In a 2008 *Chicago Tribune* newspaper story, reporters Dahleen Glanton and Stacy St. Clair explain how Obama's ancestors also valued education. Jim Robinson, Obama's great-great-grandfather, never learned to read or write. But his son, Fraser Robinson Sr., Obama's great-grandfather, did. Glanton and St. Clair write,

> Born in 1884, Fraser Sr. went to work as a houseboy for a local family before his 16th birthday. Census records show he was illiterate as a teen, but had learned to read and write by the time he had his own children.... Described by a family friend as an intelligent man who wanted his children to be well-read, Fraser Sr. always brought home his extra copies of the *Palmetto Leader* and *Grit*, a black newspaper that was popular in rural communities. "He used to make his children read those newspapers," said Margretta Dunmore Knox, who still lives in Georgetown and attended the same church as the Robinsons. "Maybe that's how they became so smart." His eldest son, Fraser Jr., was born in 1912 and graduated from high school.

Dahleen Glanton and Stacy St. Clair, "Michelle Obama's Family Tree Has Roots in a Carolina Slave Plantation," *Chicago Tribune*, December 1, 2008, www.chicagotribune. com/news/local/chi-obama-slavery-01-dec01,0,485324.story.

it. [It] was a real experiment to come here."[21] Obama's intelligence and commitment to hard work helped her excel again academically. Classmate Michelle Ealey Toliver remembers Michelle as someone who was committed to getting a good education. She says, "It was obvious that she had goals and she was going places. She didn't goof off like some other students. She was in a lot of honors classes . . . she was on a very advanced, focused track."[22] Obama was studying hard so she could be successful in life.

That attitude helped Obama become a stellar student. She made the honor roll all four years, became a member of the National Honor Society, and even took college-level classes offered by the University of Illinois. In her senior year, Obama was elected student council treasurer. She also participated in a dance program but chose not to compete in sports even though she was athletic and tall enough at nearly 6 feet (1.8m) tall to play basketball like her brother. Obama also had a boyfriend in high school. She dated David Upchurch for nearly two years.

Obama Leaves Chicago

David Upchurch grew up knowing Obama because his family lived near her South Shore home. He was Obama's boyfriend from midway through her junior year until she graduated in 1981. Although Upchurch liked Obama, he admits that he was not ready as a teenager to have a serious relationship with her or any other girl. Upchurch says, "[I] was a screw-up, plain and simple! At that point, I just didn't take my life or my future seriously. But Michelle knew what she wanted, and after graduation she was off to Princeton. I couldn't stand in her way. I wished the best for Michelle because she's always been a wonderful person."[23]

Upchurch took Michelle to the Whitney M. Young senior prom. Years later in an interview with a newspaper reporter, Upchurch said that he only had a dim recollection of the dance and could not remember if he kissed her. He said it was one of their final dates because that fall Obama left Chicago to attend Princeton University.

Chapter 2

College and A Career

If it had not been for her brother, Michelle Obama might never have attended Princeton University in Princeton, New Jersey. Princeton is one of the Ivy League schools, a small group of expensive private universities in the northeast United States whose students are mainly from rich, white families. In the early 1980s few African Americans even dreamed of attending an Ivy League school because tuition and academic standards were so high. But when Craig Robinson received an athletic scholarship to Princeton, Obama decided to go there, too. She says, "That was really my first exposure to the possibility of the Ivy League. It wasn't that I couldn't get in, or I couldn't thrive, or I couldn't survive. I didn't know to [even] want that. That wasn't the vision that I could see for myself because I couldn't see anybody around me doing that."[24]

When Obama decided on Princeton, she went to a guidance counselor at Whitney M. Young in November 1980 for help in filling out Princeton's application form. The counselor told Obama that her test scores were not high enough to get into Princeton and reluctantly helped her. Obama did not let the counselor discourage her. She believed that if her brother could go to Princeton she could, too. She says, "I knew him, and I knew his study habits, and I was, like, 'I can do that, too.'"[25] What might have kept the counselor from encouraging Obama to pursue her dream was the belief then of some people, blacks as well as whites, that African Americans did not have the social skills or intelligence to succeed at such prestigious schools.

Obama mentioned that incident often during the 2008 presidential election when she campaigned for her husband, Barack. She cited the counselor's attitude to show how preconceived expectations that people have about blacks can sometimes rob them of opportunities they should have. In an appearance in Madison, Wisconsin, Obama said,

> All my life I have confronted people who had a certain expectation of me. Every step of the way, there was somebody telling me what I couldn't do. I applied to Princeton, "You can't go there, your test scores aren't high enough." I graduated with departmental honors. And then I wanted to go to Harvard [Law School]. And that was "probably a little too tough for me." I didn't even know why they said that.[26]

Obama was accepted by Princeton; however, attending the prestigious school was not as easy as she had imagined.

Challenges at Princeton

Michelle Obama experienced few problems adapting to the integrated academic and social life at Whitney M. Young, where the black students greatly outnumbered the white students. Going to Princeton, however, proved to be a difficult challenge. Obama was one of only 94 African Americans out of the school's 1,141 freshmen students. For the first time in her life, Obama was living in a world in which there were many more white students than black students. There were also very few black teachers at Princeton.

The small group of black students felt alienated from white students. That was because some white students acted in a racist manner toward blacks or seemed ill at ease around them because they had never socialized with blacks before. Angela Acree, a college roommate of Obama's, says white students who shared classes with blacks would pretend not to recognize them outside

The campus of Princeton where Michelle Obama attended college. Obama commonly faced racism while at the university.

of class. "It was, like, here comes a black kid,"[27] Acree says of the attitude some white classmates had toward her. Two other college friends of Obama—Hilary Beard and Lisa F. Rawlings—said some white students acted in strange and insulting ways toward them. "A lot of white students there had never been around black students. They would want to touch my hair," said Beard, while Rawlings added, "I cannot tell you the number of times I was called 'Brown Sugar.'"[28]

The unease some whites felt toward blacks included Obama's first roommate—or at least her roommate's family. When Obama arrived on campus in September 1981, she shared a dormitory room with Catherine Donnelly, who was from Louisiana. When Donnelly told her family she had a black roommate, her mother was so upset that she demanded school officials move her daughter to another room and even threatened to remove her from Princeton. Donnelly, however, says she did not mind that Obama was black: "From the minute we met, I liked her. Here was a really smart black woman who I found charming, interesting and

"A Sexist, Segregated Place"

A ngela Acree was Michelle Obama's roommate for three years at Princeton. Like Obama, she often felt uncomfortable at the nearly all-white university. Acree bluntly told one magazine she believed that "it was a very sexist, segregated place." Although Princeton was founded in 1746, it did not allow women to enroll as undergraduates until 1969, only a dozen years before Obama began studying there. When Obama arrived at Princeton, the exclusive "eating clubs" for wealthier students and many social organizations on campus were still heavily biased toward males. Princeton was segregated for the first three centuries of its existence. In 1904 Princeton president Woodrow Wilson—who in 1912 would be elected president of the United States—declared proudly that no black had ever sought admission to the school. He also said he did not think any African American student could succeed at Princeton. When African American Bruce Wright was accidentally admitted in 1936, the school refused to let him attend classes. The first African Americans to attend Princeton were four students in a U.S. Navy training program during World War II— John Lee Howard, James Everett Ward, Arthur Jewell Wilson, and Melvin Murchison. In 1947 Howard, who majored in biology, was Princeton's first African American graduate. There were very few African American students after that until the 1970s when the school began recruiting them.

Quoted in Lauren Collins, "The Other Obama: Michelle Obama and the Politics of Candor," *New Yorker*, March 10, 2008, p. 92.

funny."[29] However, Donnelly moved to another room at the end of the first semester.

Obama never knew what Donnelly's family had done until 2008, when a newspaper reporter contacted her after talking to the Donnelly family. Obama's response to the reporter was "We [she and Donnelly] were never close. But sometimes that's the thing you sense, that there's something that's there [unease with blacks], but it's often unspoken."[30]

There was an economic as well as a racial barrier between students because most of the white students were from wealthy families and had much more money than Obama and other black students. The whites drove expensive cars and ate meals at exclusive on-campus "eating clubs," places in which the only blacks were usually those preparing and serving food. Obama's working-class parents could not afford her tuition, much less her expenses. In order to attend Princeton, Obama had to obtain financial aid from the school and take out student loans. For most of her four years at Princeton, Obama shared a small dormitory room with three African Americans from similar economic backgrounds. Roommate Angela Acree admits, "We were not rich. A lot of kids had TVs and sofas and furniture. We didn't."[31] But they did have lots of albums by Stevie Wonder, Obama's favorite musician.

One advantage Obama had in going to Princeton was that Craig had already been there for two years and was a star on the school's basketball team. Although his campus fame helped Michelle gain some acceptance with students, Craig claims it might have hurt her social life. He says, "When she first got to Princeton, I was still there, and I think guys wouldn't date her just because they knew I was her brother."[32]

It had been easy growing up black in Chicago because Obama had always been surrounded by other African Americans. But at Princeton, she learned what it was like to be black in a country dominated socially, economically, and politically by whites.

Finding Her Racial Identity

Obama and other black students at Princeton tended to hang out together at the Third World Center, which the school had established as a gathering place for black, Hispanic, Jewish, and Asian students. The minority students banded together because they often felt ignored or uncomfortable around white students, the majority on campus. Obama admits that the center became a safe haven for blacks students like herself. "Being one of the school's few African-American students at the time, I found there weren't

Being African American, like this Princeton student, Michelle found that there was a lack of social opportunities for minorities, so she spent most of her time studying and working.

many [social] opportunities for minorities," Obama says. "So we created a community within a community and got involved at places like the Third World Center."[33]

Although Obama and other African Americans studied and spent much of their free time at the center, they also socialized with white friends. During one spring break, Obama and two roommates joined Jewish students they knew on a ski trip to Vermont. "We were three black women on a trip with all of these white Jewish kids," Acree, says. "We stuck out like sore thumbs. But we had a great time."[34]

There was not a lot of time for having fun, however, because Obama was so busy studying and working. Students who received financial aid from the school had to work on campus to earn the money. Obama did that by coordinating an after-school day-care center at the Third World Center. "When I wasn't studying, I was working,"[35] Obama says.

Obama's experiences as a black student in a mostly white school affected her so deeply that she decided to write about race in the senior thesis that was a requirement for graduation. It was titled "Princeton-Educated Blacks and the Black Community." To write it, Obama interviewed four hundred black Princeton graduates about their experience at the school and how it had affected their racial attitudes. Obama wrote that Princeton gave blacks a quality education that helped them achieve success in their chosen fields. But she also noted that blacks often felt uncomfortable socially at Princeton and claimed those uneasy feelings were because the school seemed to care more about white students. Obama writes, "Predominately White universities like Princeton are socially and academically designed to cater to the needs of the White students comprising the bulk of their enrollments."[36] Her thesis noted that during her time at Princeton, there were only five black tenured professors and the Afro-American studies program was one of the school's smallest and most understaffed.

Obama was not afraid to point out faults in how Princeton treated black students. She was also fearless when it came to criticizing the way the school taught French. Obama was so aggressive in telling French teachers they should emphasize conversation in classes that her brother Craig became embarrassed. Obama's mother recalls, "Michelle's always been very vocal about anything. If it's not right, she's going to say so. When she was at Princeton, her brother called me and said, 'Mom, Michelle's here telling people they're not teaching French right.' She thought the style was not conversational enough. I told him, 'Just pretend you don't know her.'"[37]

Although Obama's time at Princeton showed her that some whites would snub her because of the color of her skin, she also proved to herself that she could compete intellectually with whites at one of the nation's premier schools. That gave Obama the confidence to apply to Harvard Law School, the nation's most prestigious law school.

Aware of Her "Blackness"

Michelle Obama's four years at Princeton University made her more aware of race. That was because, for the first time in her life, she was truly in a minority as she lived and went to school with many more whites than blacks. Obama left Princeton with a negative attitude about the way she had been treated there and a negative outlook on the way that a society dominated by whites would treat her. In her senior thesis, "Princeton-Educated Blacks and the Black Community," Obama writes,

> My experiences at Princeton have made me far more aware of my "Blackness" than ever before. I have found that at Princeton no matter how liberal and open-minded some of my White professors and classmates try to be toward me, I sometimes feel like a visitor on campus; as if I really don't belong. Regardless of the circumstances under which I interact with Whites at Princeton, it often seems as if, to them, I will always be Black first and a student second. These experiences have made it apparent to me that the path I have chosen to follow by attending Princeton will likely lead to my further integration and/ or assimilation into a White cultural and social structure that will only allow me to remain on the periphery of society; never becoming a full participant.

Michelle LaVaughn Robinson, "Princeton-Educated Blacks and the Black Community," senior thesis, Princeton University, 1985.

Harvard Law School

Charles J. Ogletree was Obama's adviser at Harvard. He says by the time Obama began attending Harvard in 1985, she had figured out what it meant to be an African American woman in a world dominated by whites. According to Ogletree, "Princeton was a real crossroads of identity for Michelle. [By] the time she got to Harvard she had answered the question. She could be both brilliant and black."[38] The reason Obama decided to become a lawyer was also tied into her new awareness of her racial identity. She believed she could use legal skills to help blacks and other poor people have a better life. In her Princeton senior thesis on race, she writes,

> There was no doubt in my mind that as a member of the Black community I was somehow obligated to this community and would utilize all of my present and future resources to benefit this community first and foremost. This realization has presently, made my goals to actively utilize my resources to benefit the Black community more desirable.[39]

Obama fulfilled her desire to help blacks by working for the Harvard Legal Aid Bureau. Run entirely by law students, the

Black students participate in a sit-in at Harvard Law School in 1988. Although Michelle often agreed with the causes for which the students were fighting, she never joined in the public protests.

Impressive Academic Abilities

Harvard Law School's reputation as the nation's finest law school is based on its high academic standards. In *Michelle Obama: First Lady of Hope*, author Elizabeth Lightfoot notes that Obama's fellow students and her professors were impressed with her academic abilities as a student. Lightfoot writes,

> As [her friend] Verna Williams said, Michelle was an extraordinarily intelligent and able law student, so much so that she asked her to be her partner on a mock trial case. Even back then, "she had this incredible presence," Williams said. "She could very easily be the Senator Obama that people are talking about. She's very, very smart, very charismatic, very well-spoken—all the things that Barack is." [One] of her professors, David B. Wilkins, recalled that Michelle was unusually outspoken and clear about her own opinions—again, not one to shy away from a difficult conversation. "Michelle was a student in my legal profession class, in which I ask students how they would react to difficult and professional challenges," he said. "Not surprisingly, many students shy away from putting themselves on the line this way, preferring to hedge their bets on deeply technical arguments that seem to absolve them from the responsibilities of decision making. Michelle had no time for such fig leaves. She always stated her position clearly and decisively." Randall Kennedy, another one of Michelle's professors, [called] Michelle "quiet and determined." She was "very well organized."

Elizabeth Lightfoot, *Michelle Obama: First Lady of Hope*, Guilford, CT: Lyons Press, 2009, pp. 30–31.

bureau provides legal assistance in civil cases to poor people who cannot afford lawyers. Law students usually work twenty hours a week for the bureau, a huge commitment considering how hard their studies are.

According to Ogletree, Obama worked hard to help people. He says, "She was a very diligent and tenacious student lawyer who always put her clients first."[40] Ronald Torbert, who worked at the bureau when Obama did, says students handle common legal problems, like landlord-tenant disputes and child custody disputes in divorces. Torbert agrees that Obama took her work seriously and said she worked harder than almost anyone. He says the one thing he remembers most clearly about her is that she was not impressed when other students also worked hard. He says, "You think you're working hard and I think her attitude is: 'Well, that's what you're supposed to do.'"[41]

As at Princeton, Obama belonged to several African American organizations at Harvard, like the *Harvard BlackLetter Law Journal*, whose members wrote about legal issues, and the Black Law Student Association, which was mainly a social club for African American students on the nearly all-white campus. While Obama was at Harvard, students protested the low number of black students and teachers. Although Obama had never been very interested in political causes, she went to at least one demonstration to protest for more African American faculty members. Randall Kennedy, one of Obama's professors, claims that Obama shied away from public protests because of her personality. "Michelle had a more modest, quieter, lower profile,"[42] he said. Instead of giving speeches at protests, Obama preferred to quietly recruit black undergraduates for Harvard Law from other schools to boost the number of African Americans.

Obama earned her law degree from Harvard Law School in 1988. She then returned home to Chicago to begin her career as a lawyer with Sidley and Austin, a firm known today as Sidley Austin LLP.

Obama Becomes a Lawyer

Like other firms, Sidley and Austin hired law students each summer. It did that to give the students experience and to assess their talent to see if they would be worth hiring when they graduated. Obama had worked there during the summer of 1987. The firm liked her so much that it hired her a year later and assigned her to the firm's division that dealt with marketing and copyright issues. The division's clients included companies that sold products ranging from automobiles to beer as well as some that produced various forms of entertainment including television shows.

One of Obama's first important projects was to work on legal questions regarding the marketing of *Barney*, a new children's show that became an instant hit. Even though Obama did not have experience in that area of law, Andrew Goldstein, a lawyer who worked with her, said Obama caught on quickly and did a very good job. He was also impressed with her intelligence and self-confidence, which enabled her to defend her side of any argument. Goldstein says, "You didn't want to under-estimate her."[43]

At the age of twenty-three, Obama was working as a lawyer in one of Chicago's most noted legal firms. But in the next few years, events would turn her life upside down as she took new directions in both her career and personal life.

Chapter 3

A New Career, Marriage, and Motherhood

By the summer of 1989, Michelle Robinson had settled comfortably into her new life as a lawyer for Sidley and Austin. She was happy because she had returned home to Chicago, a city she loved, and was back with her close-knit family. Michelle was doing well as a lawyer and making more money than her dad—her starting salary was $65,000 a year, almost $25,000 more than Fraser Robinson III. Newton Minow, a senior partner at Sidley and Austin, praised Michelle's work and said, "We were all crazy about her."[44]

Michelle Meets Barack

Michelle was one of fourteen African American attorneys at Sidley and Austin. In 1989 senior partners in the firm asked her to mentor Barack Obama, a first-year law student who had been hired for the summer. The partners chose Michelle because they respected her and because Barack was attending Harvard Law School, her alma mater.

Michelle knew a little about Barack before she met him. Because Sidley and Austin did not usually hire first-year law students, Michelle realized Barack must be highly intelligent to have been hired. Some of the women in the office had also told her that

Michelle met Barack Obama at the law firm they both worked at in 1989, a year before this picture of her future husband was taken.

Barack was handsome and had a great personality. But Michelle's future husband failed to impress her when they had lunch to get to know each other. She says,

> He sounded too good to be true. I had dated a lot of brothers who had this kind of [smart and charismatic] reputation going in, so I figured he was one of these smooth brothers who could talk straight and impress people. So we had lunch, and he had this bad sports jacket and a cigarette dangling from his mouth, and I thought "Oh, here you go. Here's this good-looking, smooth-talking guy. I've been down this road before."[45]

As his mentor, Michelle helped Barack get used to working in the large law firm. She educated him about various office procedures, taught him how to use the copy machine, and answered any other questions he had. Earlier that year, Michelle had told her mother that she was going to concentrate on her career and had no time for dating. Barack, however, was so attracted to Michelle that he wanted to go out with her. While he kept pestering her for a date, she kept refusing because she claimed it was not proper for her to date someone she was mentoring. Barack finally got some time alone with Michelle after a company social event. He recalls, "After a firm picnic, she drove me back to my apartment and I offered to buy her an ice cream at the Baskin-Robbins store across the street. We sat on the curb and ate our ice creams in the sticky afternoon heat. [When they finished eating] I asked if I could kiss her. It tasted of chocolate."[46]

Buying Michelle an ice cream cone did not count as a real date, but they soon went to see *Do the Right Thing*, a movie by director Spike Lee. They continued seeing each other that summer and Michelle got to know Barack better. As he talked about his past, she was amazed to learn that Barack had grown up in Hawaii and had a white mother.

His background was so different than hers that Michelle wondered if she could ever have a long-lasting relationship with him. She joked about that during a 2008 presidential campaign appearance when she told an audience how she first felt about him. She said, "I've got nothing in common with this guy. He grew up in Hawaii! Who grows up in Hawaii? He was biracial. I was like, OK, what's that about? And then it's a funny name, Barack Obama. Who names their child Barack Obama?"[47] Barack's exotic background, however, would eventually captivate Michelle just as much as it would voters two decades later.

Barack's Unique Heritage

Barack Hussein Obama Jr. was born on August 4, 1961, in Honolulu, Hawaii. He was named after his father, Barack Obama Sr., a Kenyan native. His mother, Ann Dunham, was white and had been born in Wichita, Kansas. Obama and Dunham met in 1960 while taking a Russian language class at the University of Hawaii. They fell in love and were married on February 2, 1961.

Barack Obama poses with his father at the age of ten. Obama's unique family was one of the things that Michelle found interesting about him.

When Barack Sr. finished his degree in economics, he won a scholarship to study at Harvard University. Without the money to take his family with him, Barack Sr. left Ann and their two-year-old son in Hawaii. The couple divorced in 1964 and Dunham raised her son with help from her parents, Stanley and Madelyn Dunham, who lived in Honolulu. Ann was a loving mother and Obama says, "Everything that is good about me, I think I got from her."[48] Obama only saw his father one more time, when the elder Obama visited Hawaii in December 1971.

In 1967 when Obama was six years old, his mother married Lolo Soetoro, an Indonesian student attending college in Hawaii. Obama then moved with his mother and stepfather to Soetoro's home in Jakarta, where they lived for four years. Obama then returned to Hawaii to live with his grandparents and attend Punahou Academy, an elite prep school. Despite the differences in their backgrounds, Michelle saw a common bond in how they had been raised. She says, "Both Barack and I came from similar households—not in terms of race, he came from a bi-racial fam-

One Big Traditional Family

Barack Obama loved Michelle Robinson's family. It was everything that his was not. In his book, *The Audacity of Hope: Thoughts on Reclaiming the American Dream*, Obama explains how Michelle's traditional, loving family showed him what he had missed growing up. Obama writes,

> It turned out that visiting the Robinson household was like dropping in on the set of *Leave It to Beaver* [a television show]. There was Fraser, the kindly, good-natured father, who never missed a day of work or any of his son's ballgames. There was Marian, the pretty, sensible mother who baked birthday cakes, kept order in the house, and had volunteered at school to make sure her children were behaving and that the teachers were doing what they were supposed to be doing. There was Craig, the basketball-star brother, tall and friendly and courteous and funny [and] there were uncles and aunts and cousins everywhere.... For someone like me, who had barely known his father, who had spent much of his life traveling from place to place, his bloodlines scattered to the four winds, the home that Fraser and Marian Robinson had built for themselves and their children stirred a longing for stability and a sense of place that I had not realized was there.

Barack Obama, *The Audacity of Hope: Thoughts on Reclaiming the American Dream*, New York: Crown, 2006, pp. 331–32.

ily and lived in Hawaii—the values that we were raised on were the same. There's nothing more important than family and community. That's always the priority."[49]

These shared values gave Barack a chance at winning Michelle's love, a challenge no other suitor had achieved.

Michelle and Barack's Courtship

Craig Robinson says that when Barack began dating his sister, no one in his family thought the relationship would last. That was because in the past, Michelle had always found something wrong with the men she dated and ended the relationships. Craig said that kept happening because his sister compared every man she dated with her father, who she idolized. Michelle herself admits that was true. She says she was so picky that "my parents weren't very optimistic that I was going to find anybody who would put up with me."[50]

Michelle was still unsure about Barack when he took her to a meeting of community activists in Altgeld Gardens, a poor black area. After graduating from Columbia University in 1983 with a degree in political science, Barack had worked for three years as the director of Developing Communities Project (DCP), a church-based community organization in Chicago. He helped the poor by starting a job training program, a college preparatory tutoring program, and a tenants' rights organization in Altgeld. He quit that job to attend Harvard Law School, but now he was returning to talk to people he knew there.

The meeting was in a church basement. As Barack spoke, Michelle was stunned at the eloquence and the power of the speech he delivered to poor African Americans. He told them everyone had to commit themselves to fighting to make things better for not only themselves but other people. "And as he spoke," Michelle said years later, "the room was silent, except for a few amens."[51] Michelle said it was then that she opened her heart to the man she would marry. "What I saw in him on that day was authenticity and truth and principle. That's who I fell in love with, that man,"[52] she says.

Their Relationship Turns Serious

When Michelle began to get serious about Barack, she took him home to meet her parents to see what they thought of him. She also had her brother play basketball with Barack because Craig

After maintaining a long-distance relationship, Michelle married Barack Obama on October 18, 1992, in Chicago.

Barack's Big Game

One of the tests Barack Obama had to pass to win approval of Michelle Robinson's family was to play basketball with her brother Craig, a basketball star at Princeton University. In this excerpt from a magazine article, Craig and Michelle discuss that game:

[Craig:] My sister wanted me to take him to play ball, because she heard my father and I say how you can tell a lot about a personality on the court. So, when she got serious, she said, "Take this guy and go play." We had all met him and thought he was a good guy, and she didn't fire him like the other boyfriends. He ended up being a pretty decent guy on the court. [He] wasn't selfish. He was team-oriented, and the game is self-policing when you don't have refs [referees]. He wasn't like a soft guy.

[Michelle:] Craig's opinion was important, and we're a sports family at heart. We grew up in gymnasiums and baseball fields, generally watching Craig play. Craig has always said you measure the character by what type of sportsman they are, and it was good to hear directly from my brother that [Barack] was solid and he was real and he was confident, confident but not arrogant, and a team player, something that you could sense on the court.

Quoted in Andy Katz, "Brown Coach Robinson Coaching Brother-in-Law Obama, Too," *ESPN*, September 13, 2007, http://sports.espn.go.com/ncb/columns/story?columnist=katz_andy&id=3009012.

and his father believed that people reveal their true character in athletic competition. Barack passed the test by proving he was an unselfish player and an on-court leader. "He was aggressive without being a jerk, and I was able to report back to my sister that this guy is first-rate,"[53] Robinson said. His seal of approval helped

Barack pass an important test in winning Michelle's affection.

After he returned to Harvard that fall, Barack and Michelle maintained a long-distance relationship. Although they grew closer over the next two years, Barack was hesitant about getting married and Michelle began to wonder if he would ever ask her to be his wife. Then one evening in 1991, Barack took Michelle to Gordon, an expensive Chicago restaurant. When she asked him again if they were ever going to get married, Barack ticked off a list of reasons why they should not marry, including the fact that their love for each other was more important to their relationship than a marriage certificate. His arguments continued until dessert arrived—a plate bearing a small box. When Michelle opened the box and saw an engagement ring, Barack said, "That kind of shuts you up, doesn't it?"[54] He then asked Michelle to marry him.

They were wed October 18, 1992, at Trinity United Church of Christ in Chicago. After a brief honeymoon on the West Coast, they returned to Chicago and went back to work. Michelle, however, was no longer a lawyer with Sidley and Austin.

Rethinking Her Direction

When Obama began working for Sidley and Austin, many people envied her because she was making a lot of money. However, she soon became disenchanted with her work. A big part of the change in her attitude toward her job was the death of two people she loved—her father and her Princeton roommate, Suzanne Alele. Alele died on June 23, 1990, of cancer at the age of twenty-five and Robinson died on March 6, 1991. Obama said the two deaths in such a short span of time "made me realize that I could die tomorrow. I had to ask myself, 'Is this how I want to spend my time?'"[55]

The self-doubt about the direction her life was also linked to her growing guilt about not doing something to help other African Americans. Like many students who graduate with large college debts, Obama had felt compelled to get a high-paying job so she could pay off her student loans. She had done that, but working at the law firm was contrary to her belief that educated

Why Michelle Left Sidley and Austin

When Michelle Obama left Sidley and Austin in July 1991 to work for the city of Chicago, she knew she would be taking a big pay cut. Fraser Robinson III even asked his daughter how she expected to pay off her college loans while working for Mayor Richard Daley. In her book, *Michelle: A Biography*, author Liza Mundy explores why Obama made the job switch. Mundy writes,

> When her dad died, Michelle told the *New York Times*, "I looked out at my neighborhood and sort of had an epiphany that I had to bring my skills to bear in the place that made me. I wanted to have a career motivated by passion and not just money." Explaining this to a *Chicago Sun-Times* reporter in 2004, she also expressed a lingering sense of guilt about enjoying material success while others who shared her origins and upbringing were not faring as well. She remembers asking herself, "Can I go to the family reunion in my [Mercedes] Benz and be comfortable, while my cousins are struggling to keep a roof over their heads?" Moreover, she wasn't enthralled with the work [as a lawyer], and apparently didn't think many of her colleagues were either. Explaining to *Newsweek* in 2008 why she left the firm, she said, "I didn't see a whole lot of people who were just thrilled to be there."

Liza Mundy, *Michelle: A Biography*, New York: Simon & Schuster, 2009, p. 103.

blacks should work to better life for other blacks and all poor people. Her change in attitude was undoubtedly due in part to talks she had with Barack before they married. Michelle says,

> We had many debates about how to best effect change. We both wanted to affect the community [they lived in] on a larger scale than either of us could individually, and we

wanted to do it outside of big corporations. It [their work] was not a "make a lot of money, wrap it up and call it a day" thing.[56]

Barack himself had always been committed to public service; that was why he worked as a community organizer in Chicago before attending law school. When Barack graduated from Harvard in 1991 as the first black president of the *Harvard Law Review*, he could have landed a high-paying job with any law firm in the nation. Instead, he chose positions that paid far less because he wanted to do something to help people. He first directed Illinois Project Vote, a drive that registered one hundred thousand new voters, most of them poor and minority citizens. Barack then joined a small Chicago law firm that handled civil rights cases and began teaching constitutional law at the University of Chicago Law School.

Makes a Career Change

In 1991 Obama begin searching for a job that would allow her to do something for people as well. She began writing letters to charities and government agencies about possible positions and one led to an interview with Valerie Jarrett, Mayor Richard Daley's deputy chief of staff. "I interviewed Michelle, and an introductory session turned into an hour and a half," said Jarrett. "I offered her a job at the end of the interview, which was totally inappropriate since it was the mayor's decision."[57] After Jarrett made the offer, however, Obama told her that before she could accept she wanted Jarrett to meet Barack. He was worried that Michelle might not be cut out for working in a political atmosphere and wanted to talk to her new boss. Jarrett agreed and the three met for dinner. Jarrett says, "I can remember sitting in [a restaurant] booth, with Barack on the other side, interrogating me in the nicest possible way. I can't think of many people you hire who say, 'I'd like you to meet my fiancée,' but I would have done just about anything to get Michelle."[58]

In July 1991 when Obama began working as an assistant to

Valerie Jarrett, left, was so impressed by Michelle during a job interview that she hired her on the spot.

Mayor Daley, she earned $60,000 a year, less than she had made in her first year at Sidley and Austin. But she finally had the satisfaction of a job that meant something to her.

Obama handled complaints from citizens, companies, and other government agencies. The work she did was not easy. Jarrett admits,

> Usually, when issues get to the mayor's office, they have worked their way through the bureaucracy. And the problems are sufficiently complicated that it takes somebody with a very level head and an honest broker and a sense of right and wrong and reason to sort them through. So we were looking for a person who could help us do that, and Michelle was outstanding at that.[59]

Jarrett was so impressed with Obama's work that a year later when she was named head of the Chicago Department of Planning and Development, she took Obama with her. Obama became the agency's deputy director of community development, a job that involved developing strategies and negotiating business agreements to promote and stimulate economic growth in Chicago. Although far different from and less financially rewarding than being a lawyer with a big firm, Obama preferred working in the public sector, contributing to her native city and the well-being of its citizens. Years later, Obama explained, "I did exactly what leaders in my community told me to do. They said do your best in school, work hard, study, get into the best schools you can get into and when you do that, baby, you bring that education back and you work in your communities."[60]

Michelle's Career Track

After working nearly two years for the city of Chicago, Obama got a new job. In 1993 she accepted the position of executive director of Public Allies, a nonprofit organization that encourages young people to get involved in public service. Obama took the new position even though quitting a secure job as Chicago's deputy director of community development was a gamble; she even had to take another pay cut to join Public Allies. But Obama says she did it because she was excited about the challenges the new job presented. "It sounded risky and just out there. But for some reason it just spoke to me. This was the first time I said, 'this is what I say I care about. Right here. And I will have to run it,'"[61] she explains. Obama also wanted the job because she was thrilled to be doing something directly to help poor young people, most of them poor and African American.

The nonprofit group, which is funded mainly by taxpayer dollars, was founded nationally in 1992 to groom young people for future leadership roles by training them to perform community service projects. Obama created the Chicago program from scratch. Under her leadership, Public Allies Chicago recruited young people from housing projects and youth centers as well as colleges and universities. One youth she worked with was Jose

Michelle's job as executive director of Public Allies allowed her to help underprivileged minority youth to become future leaders in their communities.

A. Rico, an illegal Mexican immigrant. When Obama asked him what his goal was, Rico said he wanted to open a high school for Latinos. She helped him get his citizenship and he eventually helped start the Multicultural Arts High School in Chicago. He also became the principal of the school. "Michelle was tough, man; she let nothing slide,"[62] he remembers.

After building perhaps the nation's strongest Public Allies program, Obama changed jobs again, accepting the position of associate dean of student services at the University of Chicago in the fall of 1996. One of her accomplishments at the university was the creation of a community-service program for undergraduate students.

Barack's Dreams

Obama's husband meanwhile was working for a small public interest firm as a civil rights attorney and he was also teaching constitutional law at the University of Chicago. Barack's dream though, was to be a public official. When he pursued this dream, it drastically changed both their lives.

Chapter 4

A Politician's Wife

Barack Obama decided to run for the Illinois State Senate in 1996. Michelle had reservations at first about his candidacy. Although Fraser Robinson III had been a Democratic Party precinct captain, the Robinson family had always been suspicious of elected officials and Michelle had once claimed that "politics is a waste of time."[63]

Her attitude had been shaped by the long, sordid history of corruption and dirty election tactics that tainted Chicago and Illinois political history. Michelle was also worried about how much money her husband would have to spend to be elected and the extra time he would be away from home to campaign while still working as a state legislator and law professor.

But the couple talked it over and Barack persuaded Michelle to let him run. She finally told him, "If that's what you really want to do, I think you'd be great at it. You're everything people say they want in their public officials."[64] Barack won the election partly due to Michelle. Because of her jobs and family connections, she knew a host of influential African American business and political leaders who supported his candidacy. Valerie Jarrett, Michelle's boss when she worked for the city, claims that "her being from Chicago, from the Southside of Chicago, was an asset to Barack in terms of enhancing his ties to the community."[65] Jarrett herself served as finance chairman for Barack's campaign.

Big Changes Underway

Life changed for the Obamas when Barack won the election. When the legislature was meeting, Barack had to spend part of each week in Springfield, the capital of Illinois. He now spent a lot of time away from home.

Then, on July 4, 1998, Michelle and Barack had their first child, a daughter they named Malia Ann. Like other new parents, the Obamas discovered it was not easy taking care of an infant who woke up often during the night. Luckily for the couple, Michelle liked going to bed early while Barack preferred staying up late. They discovered that this difference in their sleep patterns made it easier to care for their daughter. Barack explains,

Michelle holds her oldest daughter Malia while Barack gives a speech. Like other new parents, the Obamas found it difficult to tend to a newborn while both working full-time jobs.

Did Michelle Know?

Many people have questioned whether Michelle Obama knew about Barack's political ambitions before he ran for the Illinois State Senate. In the article, "When Michelle Met Barack," in the *Washington Post*, reporter Liza Mundy writes,

> Michelle has always insisted that she was unaware, early on, of Barack's political ambitions. "We didn't talk about politics specifically," she told me [in 2007]. But Obama wasn't keeping his ambitions secret. Michelle's brother, also speaking to me in 2007, recounted one of the first times Michelle brought Barack to a party that included the extended family, during which Craig [Robinson] pulled Barack aside to quiz him on his prospects. [When] Craig asked about his career plans, Barack replied, "I think I'd like to teach at some point in time, and maybe even run for public office." Craig assumed Barack wanted to run for a post like city alderman, but Barack let him know that his sights were set higher. "He said no, at some point he'd like to run for the U.S. Senate," Craig recalled. "And then he said, 'Possibly even run for president at some point.'" [The] Robinsons tended to be cynical about politics and politicians. When I related this anecdote to Michelle, she laughed as though she had not heard it before. "He probably should have said: 'Don't tell Michelle!'" she cracked, meaning that she shared her family's antipathy toward politics and implying that she didn't realize Barack had serious political aspirations.

Liza Mundy, "When Michelle Met Barack," *Washington Post*, October 5, 2008.

Suddenly our different biorhythms came in handy: while Michelle got some well-earned sleep, I would stay up until one or two in the morning, changing diapers, heating breast milk [to feed Malia], feeling my daughter's soft breath against my chest as I rocked her to sleep, guessing at her infant dreams.[66]

Malia's birth came at an ideal time for Barack because the Illinois legislature was not in session. But a few weeks later, when Barack had to return to Springfield, Michelle was left to raise Malia by herself for days at a time while also working full time. In the next few years when Barack's political career and desire to be elected to higher office kept him away from home even more, Michelle began to question whether his political ambition was fair to his family.

Obama's Success at the University of Chicago Hospitals

In the *New York Times* article, "After Attacks, Michelle Obama Looks for a New Introduction," journalists Michael Powell and Jodi Kantor explain the success Michelle Obama had in her job at the University of Chicago Hospitals. They write,

> By 2001, Mrs. Obama, married for nine years and the mother of two daughters, had taken a job as vice president of community affairs at the University of Chicago [Hospitals]. She soon discovered just how acrimonious those affairs were. Hospital brass had gathered to break ground for a children's building when African-American protesters broke in with bullhorns, drowning out the proceedings with demands that the hospital award more contracts to minority firms. The executives froze. Mrs. Obama strolled over and offered to meet later, if only the protesters would pipe down. She revised the contracting system, sending so much business to firms owned by women and other minorities that the hospital won awards. In the mostly black neighborhoods around the hospital, Mrs. Obama became the voice of a historically white institution. Behind closed doors, she tried to assuage their frustrations about a place that could seem

Raising Her Family Alone

On June 10, 2001, Michelle gave birth to Natasha, nicknamed Sasha. Although the Obamas had wanted a traditional family life in which they would both be involved in their children's lives on a daily basis, Barack was away from home for long periods working as a legislator or attending political meetings. This meant he was usually not around to eat supper with his family, read his kids a

University of Chicago Hospitals
5841 S. Maryland

Michelle's work as vice president of community affairs at the University of Chicago Medical Center was so successful that the hospital won awards.

forbidding. Like many urban hospitals, the medical center's emergency room becomes clogged with people who need primary care. So Mrs. Obama trained counselors, mostly local blacks, to hand out referrals to health clinics lest black patients felt they were being shooed away. She also altered the hospital's research agenda. When the human papillomavirus vaccine, which can prevent cervical cancer, became available, researchers proposed approaching local school principals about enlisting black teenage girls as research subjects. Mrs. Obama stopped that.

Michael Powell and Jodi Kantor, "After Attacks, Michelle Obama Looks for a New Introduction," *New York Times*, June 18, 2008, www.nytimes.com/2008/06/18/us/politics/18michelle.html?_r=1&pagewanted=1.

story, or do household chores to help Michelle. Barack says that for several years it was difficult "to balance work and family in a way that's equitable to Michelle and good for our children."[67]

His absences became more pronounced during his unsuccessful campaign for Congress in 2000 and after the birth of Sasha. Barack admits that his lack of time at home began to strain his relationship with Michelle. He says, "My failure to clean up the kitchen suddenly became less endearing. By the time Sasha was born my wife's anger toward me seemed barely contained. 'You only think about yourself,' she would tell me. 'I never thought I'd have to raise a family alone.'"[68]

After Sasha was born, Michelle decided to look for a job that was closer to home so she could better take care of her two children. She found it at the University of Chicago Hospitals, which were in the Hyde Park area where the Obamas had lived since they were married.

Michelle was still on maternity leave when she went for an interview with Michael Riordan, the hospital's president, for a position as community affairs director. She admits it turned out to be an unusual job interview because she had to take Sasha with her. She recalls, "I didn't have a babysitter. So I went in there with the stroller and did the interview. And Sasha slept through it, thank goodness."[69] Although Michelle got the job, having to take an infant to a job interview was only one of the problems she faced while trying to raise her daughters without Barack.

Coping with Guilt and Stress

The daily grind of working and caring for two young children took its toll in another way on Obama. She began to feel guilty that she was not staying at home with her children like her mother had with her and Craig. Obama admits that "every other month [since] I've had children I've struggled with the notion of 'Am I being a good parent? Can I stay home? Should I stay home? How do I balance it all?'"[70] But because Obama needed to work to help pay off their college debts and support the family, she struggled to find a way to make the situation easier for her while still giving her children the best care. Obama finally realized the solution was to quit blaming Barack and find ways to compensate for his absence. She says,

> I spent a lot of time expecting my husband to fix things, but then I came to realize that he was there in the ways he could be. If he wasn't there, it didn't mean he wasn't a good father or didn't care. I saw it could be my mom or a great baby-sitter who helped. Once I was OK with that, my marriage got better.[71]

Michelle and Barack pose for a photo with their daughters Sasha (left) and Malia. After Sasha's birth Michelle often felt guilty about working and not being home all the time for her girls.

Obama hired a full-time housekeeper to cook, clean, and do laundry. She also began depending on her mother and a circle of good friends to babysit Malia and Sasha when necessary and help out in other ways. The freedom she gained allowed Obama to exercise and spend time relaxing with her children, two things that helped her keep her sanity. Barack, who has always felt guilty about not helping more, praises Michelle for how she handled the situation: "I credit Michelle's strength—her willingness to make sacrifices on behalf of myself and the girls—with carrying us through the difficult times."[72]

But as his political ambition grew, Barack asked Michelle to make yet another sacrifice. It came when he decided to run for the U.S. Senate.

Another Political Campaign

The Obamas had gone further into debt when Barack unsuccessfully ran for Congress, so Michelle was angry a few years later when he told her he wanted to run for the U.S. Senate in 2004. Michelle was worried about money and was not sure if Barack had a chance to win such an important election. She told him, "My thing is, is this just another gamble? It's just killing us [financially]. [But] he said, 'Well, then, I'm going to write a book, a good book.' And I'm thinking, 'snake eyes there, buddy, just write a book, yeah, that's right. Yep, yep, yep. And you'll climb the beanstalk and come back down with the golden egg, Jack.'"[73]

Barack managed to persuade Michelle to allow him to try for higher office one more time, despite her skepticism. His argument was that the race would be "[one] last shot to test out my [political] ideas before I settled into a calmer, more stable, and better-paying existence."[74] And Barack's promise to write a book was not made lightly. In 1995 he had written a memoir of his life titled, *Dreams from My Father: A Story of Race and Inheritance.* So even as Obama was running for the Senate, he began writing *The Audacity of Hope*, a book that detailed his political beliefs and became a bestseller when it was published in 2006.

Barack's candidacy, which had seemed a long shot to political

Obama Says "Yes" to a Senate Race

Barack Obama has always consulted with Michelle before doing anything that would affect them and their daughters. Before Barack decided to run for the U.S. Senate in 2004, he and Michelle talked about whether he should enter the race. In his book, *Obama: From Promise to Power*, author David Mendell writes that Barack had decided he would not run if Michelle thought it was a bad idea. However, in the discussions they had, Barack used every argument he could think of to persuade her. Mendell writes,

> Explained Barack: "What I told Michelle is that politics has been a huge strain on you, but I really think there is a strong possibility that I can win this race. Obviously I have devoted a lot of my life to public service and I think that I can make a huge difference here if I won the U.S. Senate race." Added Michelle, "Ultimately I capitulated and said, 'Whatever. We'll figure it out. We're not hurting. Go ahead.'" then she laughed and told him hopefully, "And maybe you'll lose." Obama went back to [Dan] Shomon [an Obama campaign adviser] and told him he was in. "So I told Dan that I had this conversation with Michelle and she had given me the green light."

Quoted in David Mendell, *Obama: From Promise to Power*, New York: Amistad, 2007, p. 152.

experts as well Michelle, was successful. Thanks in part to support from both Chicago newspapers and Illinois senator Paul Simon, Barack won the March 2004 Democratic primary with more than 52 percent of the vote. He faced a tough opponent in the general election in Republican Jack Ryan, but Ryan withdrew from the race in June after a judge unsealed his divorce papers in response to a lawsuit brought by the media. In the documents, which were filed in 2000, Ryan's ex-wife made disturbing sexual allegations against him. In August the Republican Party replaced Ryan with Alan Keyes, a conservative black economist from Maryland who had to move to Illinois to run and was not well known by state voters.

Barack's candidacy was boosted by Ryan's departure from the election. His election effort was also strengthened by Michelle, who made several effective campaign appearances for him. In Peoria, Illinois, in October 2004 Michelle told eight hundred women that "we've [she and Barack] been guided by faith throughout the course of this political campaign—a faith that says we're all put on this Earth for a higher purpose, a faith that tells us that we can always do better."[75] Her campaign stops helped build support for Barack. But when a reporter asked her what it was like to be the wife of a candidate, Michelle responded, "It's hard, and that's why Barack is such a grateful man."[76] Although Michelle said it in a joking manner, her remark was an admission that she did not find campaigning easy and was still worried about how the election would affect her family.

Barack Becomes a Senator and a Celebrity

Barack's candidacy also received a huge boost when the Democratic Party chose him to deliver the keynote address at its convention in Boston. Because his televised speech on July 27, 2004, would be seen by tens of millions of people, Barack knew it was a chance to make himself nationally known. Michelle also knew how important the speech could be to his future. So to loosen him up before he went on-stage, Michelle hugged Barack and said, "Just don't screw it up, buddy!"[77] In his speech, Barack recounted his unique heritage and said his success story had only been possible in the United States. It was the highlight of the convention and made him an instant celebrity. It also contributed to his landslide victory over Keyes in November as he won 70 percent of the vote.

When Barack Obama was sworn in on January 4, 2005, Michelle, Malia, Sasha, and other family members watched from the Senate balcony. Afterward, six-year-old Malia asked excitedly

The Obama family poses for a picture, while Vice President Dick Cheney looks on, after Barack is sworn into office as Senator of Illinois.

"Are you a real senator now, Daddy?" and Michelle told reporters, "[Malia and Sasha are] excited. It's a big party for them."[78] Despite the festivities, however, Michelle was concerned about the overwhelming fame and growing political expectations many people had about her husband. When she and Barack voted on November 4, one man had shouted out, "We're waiting for you to be on the top of the ticket."[79] Barack had impressed so many people so deeply with his speech and landslide victory that he was being considered a possible presidential candidate in 2008.

Such predictions frightened Michelle, who worried that the unreasonable expectations could hurt him and their family. She tried to caution people by telling them not to expect too much of Barack. She said,

> Maybe one day he will do something to warrant all this attention. The only thing I'm telling people in Illinois is that 'Barack is not our savior.' I want to tell the whole country and I will if I get the opportunity. There are many of us who want to lay all of our wishes, fears, and hopes at the feet of this young man, but life doesn't work that way and certainly politics doesn't work that way.[80]

Despite her comments, an entire nation would turn to Barack Obama a few years later for answers to the tremendous problems facing the United States.

Chapter 5

On a Fast Track to the White House

B arack Obama moved to Washington, D.C., alone when he became a U.S. senator. He spent Monday through Thursday in the nation's capital and then flew home to be with his family for the weekend. The Obamas decided not to move the whole family to Washington, D.C., because Michelle wanted to keep working and they did not want to disrupt the lives of Malia and Sasha. In December 2005, near the end of Barack's first year in office, Michelle told a newspaper reporter, "We made a good decision to stay in Chicago, to remain based in Chicago, so that has kept our family stable. There has been very little transition for me and the girls. Now he's commuting a lot, but he's the grown-up. He's the senator. He can handle it. That's really helped in keeping us grounded."[81]

By then, however, Barack was considered a leading Democratic candidate for president in 2008. His speech at the 2004 Democratic National Convention had introduced him to the nation, and he had become even more popular since then because of his stands on political issues, such as the Iraq War. When a reporter asked Michelle how she felt about Barack running for president, she said she did not think her husband would enter the race. However, Michelle was pragmatic enough to admit that anything in politics is possible. "You have to wait and see what happens, what the future holds and what makes sense. Timing is everything."[82] That future came more quickly for her husband than Michelle could ever imagine.

An Unselfish Choice

At the end of 2006, Barack faced the most important decision of his life—whether he should run for president. Many political leaders and citizens were urging him to be a candidate but he was not sure if it was a good idea. In December when the family went to Hawaii for their traditional Christmas vacation, he and Michelle discussed the subject during their long walks on the beach. "Her initial instinct was to say no,"[83] Barack admits.

Michelle's hesitation arose from her fears that the campaign could harm her family. She knew Barack would be subjected to harsh political attacks by his opponents and that the campaign would disrupt their lives in many ways. Michelle also worried

Michelle waves to supporters during a campaign rally on February 11, 2007. She did not realize that campaigning for her husband would make her a political star.

A Difficult Decision

In an interview with journalist Leslie Bennetts, Michelle Obama explains how hard it was for her to agree to let Barack run for president:

> This was a sudden decision. He had just won his U.S. Senate seat. In my mind, it was "O.K., here we are—you're a U.S. senator. [I] thought, Uhhhh—you're kidding! It was like, No, not right now—right?" There was a period of "Let's not do this now; let's press the 'easy' button! Can we get a break, please?" So we had to talk about it. Before I signed on, I had to know, in my mind and my heart, how is this going to work for me, and would I be O.K. with that? He wouldn't have done this if he didn't feel confident that I felt good about it, because it is a huge sacrifice. The pressure and stress on the family isn't new. But we entered this thing knowing it was going to be really, really hard. For us, the question was: are we ready to do something really hard again, right after doing something that was really hard?

Quoted in Leslie Bennetts, "Change Agent: First Lady in Waiting," *Vanity Fair*, December 27, 2007, www.vanityfair.com/politics/features/2007/12/michelle_obama200712?currentpage=1.

that Barack would be assassinated by racists who did not want an African American president. Her fear was not unfounded. Barack did receive death threats, and the Secret Service began protecting Obama and his family on May 7, 2007, more than a year before the election and the earliest a presidential candidate had ever received such security.

Michelle knew Barack would not run if she said no, so she considered every factor before deciding. She says, "I took myself down every dark road you could go on, just to prepare myself before we jumped out there. Are we emotionally [ready] for this? I dreamed out all the scenarios."[84] Michelle finally realized she had to say yes. "Eventually," she says, "I thought, this is a smart man with a good heart, and if the only reason I wouldn't want him to be president is that I'm married to him, no, I can't be that selfish."[85]

Michelle, however, forced Barack to make some concessions in return. She told him he could not neglect their children—during the campaign he used a laptop computer with a camera so Malia and Sasha could see him during their frequent Internet telephone calls—and he had to quit smoking. Michelle told Barack it was not right for someone running for president to have that unhealthy addiction. She also made him promise that if he won the election, he would get his daughters a dog, which they badly wanted.

Barack announced his candidacy on February 10, 2007, in Springfield, Illinois. Michelle knew she would have to campaign extensively for him because the race was important. Michelle did not realize, however, that by doing so she would become a political star.

On the Campaign Trail

Since 2005, Michelle had been executive director for community affairs at University of Chicago Hospitals, a position that paid $316,000 annually. When Barack announced his candidacy, she agreed to work only part-time even though she enjoyed her job. Michelle cut back her hours to devote herself to campaigning and caring for her daughters, who would see their father even less while he was campaigning around the nation.

One of Michelle's first campaign duties came on February 11, 2007, when she and Barack appeared on the television show *60 Minutes* after he announced his intention to run. Michelle answered questions intelligently. She also displayed the playful side of her personality which endeared her to many people. She asked viewers to help her make sure Barack was quitting cigarettes. She said, "Please, America, watch. Keep an eye on him, and call me, if you see him smoking."[86] Most viewers had not known much about Michelle before that interview, but they came away

Hillary Clinton was Barack Obama's main rival for the Democratic Party nomination; Michelle Obama helped to persuade voters that Barack would be the better choice.

with a positive opinion of her.

Barack entered the race eleven months before the first primary because more than a half dozen other candidates were vying for his party's nomination. His biggest rival was New York senator Hillary Clinton, whose husband, Bill, was president from 1993 to 2001. The Clintons were a formidable political team; her campaign had already won the support of many party officials and raised millions of dollars in campaign funds. Barack was the first black candidate and Hillary was the first female candidate in U.S. history to have such a good chance to be elected president, and many Democrats were disappointed that two historic candidates were battling each other for the nomination.

Democrats had always been more open to electing a woman president, which made Clinton's candidacy appealing to many, especially women. During the campaign, Michelle emerged as a powerful weapon to counter Clinton's appeal and help persuade women to vote for her husband.

Obama Impresses Voters

Although Obama had never liked politics, she made successful appearances around the country. She was especially effective in talking to other working mothers. In Austin, Texas, in August 2007, she said,

> I don't know about you, but as a mother, wife, professional, campaign wife, whatever it is that's on my plate, I'm drowning. And nobody's talking about these issues. In my adult lifetime, I felt duped. People told me, "You can do it all. Just stay the course, get your education and you can raise a child, stay thin, be in shape, love your man, look good and raise healthy children." That was a lie.[87]

As Obama talked, women in the audience nodded their heads in agreement and sometimes laughed. She repeated her story over and over again in other cities. After her speech in New Hampshire in December 2007, Lisa Eberhart, a mental health therapist, admired Michelle for facing the same problems she did. She said, "She's lived a life that involves juggling career and raising kids. Michelle Obama emphasizes family life."[88] Michelle's ability to connect with other women helped Barack compete with Clinton for female voters.

She was so effective and popular that Barack began describing her as the "love of my life, the rock of the Obama family [and] the closer on the campaign trail."[89] He felt Michelle was a closer because she was able to persuade people to vote for him. One woman Michelle convinced was the wife of the Wapello County Democratic Party chairman in Iowa. After Michelle spoke in Ottumwa, Iowa, in December 2007, the woman told her, "I was totally between John Edwards and Barack Obama, and you sold me" to which Michelle responded, "That's my job."[90]

Michelle Obama was also good in appearances on television and radio shows. After she was interviewed on the television show *Larry King Live* in February 2008, a television political analyst gushed about how impressive she had been. "What a home run!" said Paul Begala. "Somebody needs to make a button that

Interviewing Michelle Obama

Author David Mendell interviewed Michelle Obama when he wrote a biography of her husband. In the book, *Obama: From Promise to Power*, he writes about how much she impressed him:

> Having previously interviewed wives (and husbands) of political candidates, I was uncertain what to expect. Some spouses, fearful of a verbal gaffe [mistake], are heavily scripted by campaign aides, equally fearful of a blunder. Others are more at ease with their own words but are still generally cautious in their approach. Michelle Obama exuded neither quality. She was not the least bit scripted. As with her husband, one of her strengths is the ability to put others at ease in her presence. She answered my questions in such an unhurried and relaxed fashion that she seemed only mildly calculating, if at all. I found her to be comfortable with herself, personable, intellectually engaging and deeply committed to her husband. She knew that he badly wanted to win this election [the 2004 U.S. Senate race]. Toward that end, she was adept at pointing out his positive traits; and yet she seemed to have little interest in putting an artificial gloss on her husband's foibles and faults. [Our] interview ran almost two hours, at which time I ended the session. I [came away] with the impression of a woman who was confident in her own skills, confident in her marriage and her own career and also highly respectful of her husband.

David Mendell, *Obama: From Promise to Power*, New York: Amistad, 2007, p. 98.

says 'vote for Michelle's Husband.' I support Hillary, but what a star! So poised."[91] Obama had become a political star in her own right. But like every political figure, she made some mistakes.

Her Biggest Blunder

On February 18, 2008, in Milwaukee, Wisconsin, Michelle made her biggest blunder of the campaign. "For the first time in my adult lifetime," she said, "I am really proud of my country, and not just because Barack has done well, but because I think people are hungry for change."[92] Republicans criticized Obama for not loving the United States until it looked like voters might elect her husband president. One of the most stinging responses came from Cindy McCain. McCain's husband, Senator John McCain, would eventually win the Republican Party's presidential nomination. At a Republican rally, McCain said she had always been proud of the United States, a comment that implied Michelle was not patriotic. There were so many attacks that Barack complained about them, saying, "I would never think of going after somebody's spouse in a campaign."[93]

It was not the first time Michelle had said something that some people did not like. In discussing the nation's bitter political mood she repeatedly said the United States had become a mean coun-

Michelle Obama delivering a campaign speech on behalf of her husband on February 18, 2008, where she was criticized by Republicans for her remarks.

try, something with which many people agreed. David Axelrod, Barack's top political strategist, admitted Michelle's comments sometimes created problems. "Occasionally, it gives campaign people heartburn,"[94] Axelrod said. But he also said Michelle was simply being honest about how she felt. Michelle agreed with that assessment. She said, "My view on this [criticism] is I'm just trying to be myself, trying to be as authentic as I can be. I can't pretend to be somebody else."[95]

Republicans fabricated some of the controversy. The most blatant attempt to stir up ill will against Michelle came after Barack accepted his party's nomination at the Democratic National Convention on August 26, 2008. When Barack and Michelle met on stage, they bumped fists, a celebratory gesture many blacks and athletes use. Some Republicans labeled it a "terrorist" gesture of triumph, a silly claim that no one believed.

Michelle ignored the attacks, most of which did no harm to her or Barack's campaign. She was more concerned about how the campaign was affecting her daughters.

"Our Kids First"

Barack's campaign created many changes for Malia and Sasha. In December 2007, the family skipped its Hawaii vacation so Michelle and Barack could campaign in Iowa. "When I told my 9-year-old [Malia] that we would be in Iowa, she cried,"[96] Michelle said. That bothered Michelle even though Barack won the February 3, 2008, primary over Clinton. Michelle also began to fear that the campaign could harm her daughters in other ways. It was a topic Michelle brought up in her campaign appearances. In July 2007 she told a crowd, "We are doing fine as a family. That's one of the things that people want to know most from me as the wife of the candidate: How are we holding up? We're doing our best to keep our kids first. Our view is that if our children aren't sane and whole and focused, then we can't represent that to the rest of the country."[97]

To make her daughters' lives more normal, Michelle spent as much time as possible with them because Barack was always traveling. She took them to their regular activities—soccer, dance, and drama classes for Malia, gymnastics and tap dancing for Sasha, and tennis and piano for both. To maintain such a schedule she not only cut her working hours again but kept her campaign trips short, usually being away for just one day. Michelle explains,

> I get them to a neighbor's if I can't get them to school. I get on a plane. I come to a city. I do several events. I get on a plane. I get home before bedtime. And by doing that, yeah, I'm a little tired at the end of the day, but the girls, they just think Mommy was at work. They don't know I was in New Hampshire. Quite frankly, they don't care.[98]

Malia and Sasha Make an Appearance

Obama also accommodated her daughters when they joined her on the campaign trail. On July 4, 2007, the entire family campaigned in Oskaloosa, Iowa. Obama told the audience she had refused a request by campaign coordinators to come to Iowa to campaign a day early because Sasha and Malia wanted to attend a haunted trails event at their summer camp. "Family is first for us and it will always be that way,"[99] she said.

The Obamas never forced the girls to do things for the campaign. After Barack won more states than Clinton on Super

Tuesday, February 5, 2008, when twenty-four states voted, the girls attended a victory celebration in Chicago. When Barack asked them if they wanted to come onstage, Malia told him, "Now, you know, Daddy, that's not my thing." The Obamas did not force her to face the huge, cheering crowd but Michelle noted that "the little one [Sasha] is much more interested in the limelight. And she likes to wave."[100]

The Obama family relaxes in their campaign RV after attending a campaign event in Oskaloosa, Iowa, on July 4, 2007. Even during the presidential campaign, Michelle and Barack put their daughters' needs first.

Malia and Sasha and the Campaign

In a television interview in 2007, Michelle Obama explained how she tried to protect Malia and Sasha during the campaign:

> We've tried not to let this campaign interfere with their lives. They don't have a lot of questions about it, I mean, they understand politics. Barack has had a political life ever since they were born, that's all they've known. So they're familiar, and they understand the election process, they understand what the president does, they understand the process, but they're nine and six, so they're mostly concerned about what they're going to be for Halloween, who's coming to their pot luck, you know, and we like that. We allow them to come in and out of the campaign as they choose. So, if they want to come somewhere, and they're free, they come. But usually they want to stay in their world, in their lives. They want to be with their friends, and we allow that to happen. So they don't feel like this process is taking over their lives. And they have said that they appreciate the fact that they have friends and teachers who could care less about this. My oldest daughter, actually, told her [teacher], "That's what I like about you, Miss Bikelson, you don't really care about this, and you treat me the same, no matter what."

Michelle Obama, interview by Mika Brzezinski, *Morning Joe*, *MSNBC.com*, November 13, 2007, www.msnbc.msn.com/id/21771034.

Even while on the campaign trail, Sasha (left) and Maila (right) wanted to be treated just like normal children.

Malia and Sasha did make an appearance on August 25, 2008, at the Democratic National Convention. After Obama gave a nationally televised speech about her background and why she believed Barack should be elected, they joined her onstage. Barack was not in the convention center, but when he appeared via satellite on a giant screen television to praise Michelle's speech, Malia and Sasha shouted "Love you Daddy!"[101] Their joyous greeting was a highlight of the night. But Malia was sad afterward because her father had not been there in person. Michelle said, "[Malia] cried, because she really misses him and worries about him when he's away from home for such long periods of time. Moments like that one are the most difficult for me when it comes to the girls."[102]

Michelle received vital help from her mother during the campaign to care for Malia and Sasha. To make it easier for Michelle to be away, Marian Robinson retired from a part-time job in the summer of 2007 to spend more time with her grandchildren. In February 2008, Michelle told voters in Chillicothe, Ohio, "I am standing here breathing in and out with any level of calm because my 70-year-old [mother] is home with my girls. There's nothing like grandma."[103]

Because Obama knew the campaign was not harming her daughters, she was able to crisscross the nation for nearly two years. She visited Iowa, New Hampshire, and other states repeatedly throughout 2007. When Barack won the first primary in Iowa on February 3, 2008, he became the front-runner, a position he did not relinquish. Michelle was on the road throughout the long primary season right up to the November 4 election when Barack scored a landslide victory over John McCain.

Savoring Victory

Michelle Obama made more solo appearances than any other presidential candidate's spouse ever. She also regularly drew large, enthusiastic crowds of a thousand or more people, making her the most popular and effective campaign spouse in presidential election history. So it was fitting that she shared the spotlight with Barack on election night during a rousing, emotional celebration at Grant Park in Chicago, which was only a few miles from the family's Hyde Park home.

The Obamas strode on stage arm in arm with their children to the thunderous cheers of tens of thousands of people. When Barack and Michelle kissed, the love they had for each other was apparent to the entire world.

Chapter 6

Life as the First Lady

When Barack Obama took the oath of office to become the 44th president of the United States on January 20, 2009, he placed his hand on the same Bible Abraham Lincoln used in 1861. Holding the Bible during the ceremony was Michelle, who had campaigned so hard to help him get elected. The Obamas attended ten inaugural balls that night and at each they danced to "At Last," a soulful love song made famous by legendary blues singer Etta James. Their first was the Neighborhood Ball at the Walter E. Washington Convention Center. When they arrived, a grinning Barack greeted the crowd of several hundred people by proudly asking them, "First of all, how good looking is my wife?"[104] With pop star Beyoncé singing the lyrics to "At Last," the couple danced cheek to cheek to their favorite song.

People at the ball were impressed by how graceful and elegant the Obamas looked and how much they seemed to love each other. Even celebrities watching were awed. Shakira said, "It was so emotional. It was something to tell my children about."[105] And the popular singing star from Colombia does not even have any children yet.

Michelle made no public comments on Inauguration Day so Barack could have the spotlight to himself. But that quickly changed because Michelle was now going to be the nation's First Lady, a position that made her one of the world's most famous people—the news media would now be recording her every word and action.

The Role of First Lady

The position of First Lady is not an official one in the U.S. government; the First Lady is not elected, does not get paid a salary, and has no official duties. However, the wife of the president is a very important person because she is considered a representative of the United States in her own country and around the world. The title first gained widespread use in 1877 during the inauguration of Rutherford B. Hayes when newspaper reporter Mary C. Ames referred to Lucy Webb Hayes as "the First Lady of the Land." The First Lady always serves as hostess with the president at social gatherings at the White House and frequently accompanies him on travels when it is appropriate. First Ladies usually become involved in charitable causes and some have embraced nonpolitical issues, such as the need to stop littering (Lady Bird Johnson) and literacy (Laura Bush). The first wife of a president to become actively involved in political matters was Eleanor Roosevelt, who openly advocated the cause of workers' rights and the need to fight poverty. She also traveled with U.S. soldiers during World War II and wrote a daily newspaper column. President Bill Clinton gave his wife, Hillary, a formal role in his administration to develop reforms to the nation's health-care system. The attempt failed but she continued to be involved in various policy proposals and traveled to foreign countries as a representative of the State Department.

The Next Jackie O?

Newspapers, magazines, television stations, and Web sites were intrigued by Michelle Obama for many reasons. She was not only the first African American First Lady, but she had more work experience than any other presidential spouse. They were also captivated by her beauty and flair for clothes. The day after the inauguration, there was a flood of stories in the media about

The white silk gown that Michelle wore to the inaugural balls has led to her being labeled one of the most fashionable first ladies in recent years.

A Fashion-Setting First Lady

Michelle Obama is often compared to former First Lady Jacqueline Kennedy, who wore clothes elegantly. Since becoming First Lady, Obama has been praised and criticized for how she dresses. Although most fashion critics give her high marks for style, some have attacked her for wearing a sleeveless dress for her official photograph as First Lady. In an article in the March 2009 edition of *Vogue* magazine, Obama discusses her taste in clothes and how she ignores fashion criticism:

> "I love clothes," she admits. "First and foremost, I wear what I love. What I love. That's what women have to focus on: what makes them happy and what makes them feel comfortable and beautiful. If I can have any impact, I want women to feel good about themselves and have fun with fashion." [Obama was criticized for wearing a black sweater over a fashionable dress the night her husband won the presidential election on November 4, 2008.] "I'm not going to pretend that I don't care about it. But I also have to be very practical. In the end, someone will always not like what you wear—people just have different tastes. Some will think that a sweater was horrible, [but] I was cold; I needed that sweater!"

Quoted in Andre Leon Talley, "Leading Lady," *Vogue*, March 2009, p. 501.

Obama's clothes. During the inauguration, she wore a striking dress and coat of an unusual yellow-gold color that sparkled in the sunshine; for the balls she donned a white silk gown with small flowers and light-reflecting crystals. Most observers claimed Obama looked stylish in both outfits. In an article for a newspaper in London, England, reporter Liz Jones writes, "Isn't she lovely?" and then answers the question in the affirmative. Jones also quotes Suzanne Cvetas, an English fashion expert, who claims,

"She'll be the next Jackie O."[106]

Jackie O. was Jacqueline Kennedy, wife of President John F. Kennedy (JFK). She became known as Jackie O. when she married Aristotle Onassis after JFK was assassinated in Dallas, Texas, on November 22, 1963. During Kennedy's three years as president, Jacqueline established herself as the most elegant and fashionable First Lady ever. Even before Barack was elected, some reporters were already writing that Michelle would be a worthy successor to Jacqueline's legacy. Many reporters were also comparing Barack to John Kennedy because of his eloquent speaking style and intellectual mind. Some historians have romanticized Kennedy's brief presidency as Camelot, a reference to the mythical rule of King Arthur of England. When Barack was elected, some reporters predicted he and Michelle might create something similar, called Obamalot. According to Laurence Leamer, the author of several books on the Kennedys, the comparison is justified. He says, "Men wanted to be like JFK and women wanted to be like Jackie. There hasn't been a president who has done that since JFK and Jackie. And I think President Obama and Michelle Obama may come close to that."[107]

Negative Coverage

The extensive media coverage Michelle Obama receives is not always positive. For example, she held the Lincoln Bible for several minutes while waiting for Barack to take the oath of office. A few political commentators and talk show hosts, mostly those who disagreed with Barack's policies, claimed she held it too casually while talking to other people before the ceremony. The criticism seemed silly to many people, but it showed how brightly the spotlight was shining now on the new First Lady.

And although Obama has been generally praised for how she dresses, she has drawn criticism for wearing so many sleeveless dresses. Jackie Kennedy also wore sleeveless dresses and Letitia Baldrige, Kennedy's social secretary and chief of staff when she was First Lady, has defended Obama. Baldrige says, "I think she's simply dressing to show off one of her greatest physical

Michelle has been compared to former First Lady Jackie Kennedy for many reasons, especially because they both liked to wear sleeveless dresses.

attributes—her arms. How many women her age have arms like that? I look in the mirror at my own arms and want to shoot myself."[108] Obama has toned, muscular arms because she works out often and most other women feel she is right to proudly display them.

The Obamas also remind people of the Kennedys because they have small children like the Kennedys did. People around the world found the White House antics of the Kennedy children, Caroline and John, heart-warming and the Kennedys seemed more like regular people because they had children. Gretchen Monahan, a television fashion critic, claims ten-year-old Malia and seven-year-old Sasha, were the hit of the inauguration. "I have to give my star to the girls," she said. "They were just picture perfect, smiling and happy. As a couple and a family, it makes us believe in the American ideal."[109] One of the cutest inauguration photographs shows a smiling Sasha giving her dad a thumbs-up gesture after his swearing-in ceremony.

Mom in Chief

During the 2008 presidential campaign, especially after it became apparent Barack would win, reporters asked Michelle what she would do as First Lady. She always answered that her most important job would be "mom in chief," a takeoff on the military title of commander in chief, a position the president of the United States holds has as the head of U.S. military forces. When one reporter asked her to explain the title, Michelle said, "What I meant is that my first priority would be my two girls—making sure they're happy and comfortable during what would be a major transition for them."[110] Michelle knew that moving to Washington, D.C.; living in the White House; attending a new school; and making new friends would be difficult for her daughters and that she needed to help them make the transition.

Michelle started that process after Barack was elected by going to Washington, D.C., to select a school for them. After she chose Sidwell Friends School, Obama said, "I like to be a presence in my kids' school. I want to know the teachers; I want to know the other parents."[111] She fulfilled that desire in March 2009 when she and Barack visited Sidwell for a parent-teacher conference for second-grade student Sasha.

Another major concern Obama has is helping Malia and Sasha get used to living in the White House, a huge, ornate residence that can be an imposing place for young children. Living there is even more intimidating because the family is always surrounded by Secret Service agents. When one journalist was interviewing Michelle, he noticed armed guards on the White House roof. Michelle told him nonchalantly that guards always patrol the roof. Secret Service agents also guard the Obamas whenever they

One adjustment the Obamas have had to make after becoming the First Family is always being surrounded by security. Here, a secret service agent escorts Michelle as she walks Sasha to school.

travel. They have even given each family member a code name. Barack is Renegade; Michelle is Renaissance; Malia is Radiance; and Sasha is Rosebud.

Making the White House Home

To make the White House feel more like home, the Obamas had a swing set built on the White House lawn; Malia and Sasha reportedly yelled with delight when they saw it. Another touch of home is the presence of their grandmother. Obama convinced her seventy-one-year-old mother to live with the family. "The girls are going to need her, as part of their sense of stability,"[112] Michelle said. The White House will also feel like home because Malia and Sasha still have to make their beds, clean their rooms, and clear dishes from the dinner table. Even though White House staffers would gladly do it for them, Obama believes her daughters need to learn to take care of themselves, just as she did while growing up in Chicago.

The best part of the transition for Michelle, Malia, and Sasha is that Barack now works at home most days in the White House. The Oval Office where he works is not that far from the family's private living quarters, which means they can see him much more often than in the past. Michelle explains, "We have dinner as a family together every night, and Barack, when he's not traveling, tucks the girls in [bed]. We haven't had that kind of time together for [years] so that explains a lot why we all feel so good in this space."[113]

Michelle used to text Barack often during the day to stay in touch with him. Now Michelle says "I'll just pop over and say hi."[114] Many times those visits concern Michelle's many and varied duties as First Lady.

Learning to Be First Lady

Except for hosting White House social events and traveling with the president to foreign countries, First Ladies do not have any assigned duties. Although some First Ladies have been content

Raising Children in the White House

In a 2009 interview with talk show host Oprah Winfrey, Michelle Obama explains how she fits being a mother into her busy schedule. She also explains how she is trying to give Malia and Sasha a normal childhood while growing up in the White House by making them do chores. Obama says,

> My day is structured so that I'm usually not working until 10 or 11 [A.M.]. That gives me time to get the girls out of the house. My mom is taking them to school because it's less of a scene for her [meaning reporters or photographers do not usually follow her]. With all the security involved, it's a more normal experience for them when I don't go. After I see the girls off [to school], I usually work until 3 or 4 [P.M.]. Then they're back and we start in on their homework. Then Dad comes home and we have dinner. . . . I want the kids to be treated like children, not little princesses. I told [White House staff] that they should make their beds, they should clean their plates, they should act respectfully—and that if anyone on the staff sees differently, they should come to me. So the girls help set the table, they help bring the food out, and they're in the kitchen laughing and making toast in the morning. And everyone has adjusted to the rules. Now I joke with the staff: "Don't spoil them—spoil Mom!"

Quoted in Oprah Winfrey, "Oprah Talks to Michelle Obama," *O the Oprah Magazine*, April 2009, p. 144.

with staying in the background, others have been active in promoting their own projects; some have even become involved in political and policy issues. In February when a teenager at the Adams Morgan services center for Latino families asked Obama what it was like to be First Lady, she admitted, "I think I'm still trying to figure that out."[115] But even while Obama is still learning how to do her new job, she has been a very active First Lady.

In her first month Michelle Obama visited five federal agencies to meet federal workers; lunched with Washington, D.C., mayor Adrian Fenty; went to the ballet with her family at the Kennedy Center; and hosted an African American History Month event at the White House. Michelle also gave a series of interviews to newspaper and magazine reporters anxious to know what White House life was like for the Obama family. The interviews, mothering her daughters, and her many appearances kept Obama very busy. To help Obama coordinate her schedule, handle correspondence, plan White House social events, and deal with the news media, she has a staff of twenty people.

One of the first events Obama's staff helped her coordinate was on February 11 when she presented the State Department's

Michelle greets the members of the Department of Transportation after delivering a speech on February 20, 2009. In her first month as First Lady Michelle was busy meeting with federal agencies about working with her husband's administration.

Award for International Women of Courage to seven women from Afghanistan, Guatemala, Iraq, Malaysia, Niger, Russia, and Uzbekistan. Obama said that the seven who fought for women's rights in their countries had important lessons to teach other women. She stated, "One, that as women, we must stand up for ourselves. The second, as women, we must stand up for each other. And finally, as women, we must stand up for justice for all."[116] During the ceremony at the U.S. State Department, Obama shared the stage with former First Lady Hillary Clinton, now President Obama's secretary of state.

On February 25, Obama hosted one of her first big White House social events. It was a dinner honoring soul singer Stevie Wonder, who received the Library of Congress's Gershwin Prize, the nation's highest honor for a musician. Obama said Wonder was "a man whose music and lyrics I fell in love with when I was a little girl."[117] Obama even admits that the first record album she bought was Wonder's 1972 classic *Talking Book*.

Serving the Country

Many of the ceremonies and appointments Obama made took her out of the White House. When she visited St. Mary's Center for Maternal and Child Care in early February to talk to teenagers about what they wanted to do in the future, a reporter asked her why she was visiting so many places in Washington, D.C. Obama said, "We [she and Barack] were taught that you have to get to know the community that you're in, and you have to be a part of that community, you have to get to know it in order to actively engage in it."[118] She and Barack did that together when they went to a local school to read to young children.

Michelle Obama also traveled around the country. One of her first trips as First Lady was for a cause Obama had embraced during the presidential campaign—military families. On March 13 she went to Fort Bragg in North Carolina to meet with members of the military and their families. Many military families had been experiencing financial, emotional, or physical problems due to the involvement of loved ones in the wars in Afghanistan and

Michelle signs an autograph for a U.S. soldier during a visit to Fort Bragg where she told military families that the U.S. government needs to provide them with more financial, emotional, and physical support.

Iraq. Michelle believes the federal government needs to provide more help to military families to deal with such problems. She says, "I think that's one of my jobs, is to try and shed some light on some of these issues, to not just be in that conversation with the military spouses and hear those stories, but to take that information back to the administration, to share it with the nation, so that we can think again about how we can better support these families."[119]

And as always, Obama is a trusted adviser to her husband. The couple has always discussed political issues and Barack values her opinion. During the campaign when a reporter asked Michelle if she ever counseled Barack, Michelle answered that if her husband asked for her advice, "do you expect me to hold my tongue?"[120] Michelle continues to give Barack advice even though he is president. And that is fine even with people like Fred Barnes, a conservative Republican talk show host. He says, "I have nothing against her having a policy role in the administration. Just be transparent about it and let people know that's what she's doing. Unlike the [Ronald] Reagan administration, where Nancy Reagan played a big role and denied it."[121] It was not known until years later than Reagan's wife influenced him heavily on decisions he made as president.

Living in the Present

In her first few months as First Lady, Obama is just trying to understand her new responsibilities and do them as best she can. In fact, that is always how she has lived her life. During the campaign, a reporter asked her what she expects the future to hold for her. Michelle answered, "What I know is that life changes and I never see one set of decisions as permanent. I look at it as this is what I'm doing for this time and make sense at this time in my life and I don't try to predict what the future will hold in terms of those types of decisions."[122]

It was a realistic answer because no one can know what the future holds for Michelle Obama.

Notes

Introduction: A First Lady Like No Other

1. Quoted in Darlene Superville, "First Lady Hosts Black History Month Celebration," Associated Press, February 18, 2009, http://abcnews.go.com/Politics/wireStory?id=6909389.
2. Quoted in "First Lady Michelle Obama Delivers Remarks to Youths Visiting the White House," political transcript, Federal Document Clearing House, February 18, 2009.
3. Quoted in Diane Ravitch, *The American Reader: Words That Moved a Nation*, New York: HarperCollins, 1991, p. 20.
4. Quoted in Shailagh Murray, "Michelle Obama Learns About Her Slave Ancestors, Herself and Her Country," *Washington Post*, October 2, 2008.
5. Quoted in Murray, "Michelle Obama Learns About Her Slave Ancestors, Herself and Her Country," *Washington Post*, October 2, 2008.
6. Quoted in Richard Wolffe, "Barack's Rock," *Newsweek*, February 25, 2008, p. 29.
7. Quoted in Christi Parsons, "Michelle Obama's Work-Life Balance Message Offers Insight Into Her Role as First Lady," *Chicago Tribune*, February 26, 2009.

Chapter 1: Growing Up in Chicago

8. Quoted in Liza Mundy, *Michelle: A Biography*, New York: Simon & Schuster, 2009, p. 20.
9. Quoted in Lauren Collins, "The Other Obama: Michelle Obama and the Politics of Candor," *New Yorker*, March 10, 2008, p. 92.
10. Quoted in David Colbert, *Michelle Obama: An American Story*, New York: Houghton Mifflin Harcourt, 2009, p. 17.
11. Michelle Obama, "Michelle Obama's Remarks at the Democratic Convention," *New York Times*, August 25, 2008, http://elections.nytimes.com/2008/president/conventions/videos/transcripts/20080825_obama_speech.html.
12. Quoted in Wolffe, "Barack's Rock," p. 28.
13. Quoted in Colbert, *Michelle Obama*, p. 17.
14. Quoted in Karen Springen, "First Lady in Waiting," *Chicago Magazine*, October 2004, www.chicagomag.com/Chicago-

Magazine/October-2004/First-Lady-in-Waiting.

15. Quoted in Sharon Churcher, "Mrs O: The Truth About Michelle Obama's 'Working Class' Credentials," *Daily Mail* (London), February 23, 2008, www.dailymail.co.uk/femail/article-517824/mrs-o-the-truth-michelle-obamas-working-class-credentials.html.

16. Quoted in Sandra Sobieraj Westfall, "Michelle Obama: This Is Who I Am," *People*, June 18, 2007.

17. Quoted in Wolffe, "Barack's Rock," p. 29.

18. Quoted in Rebecca Johnson, "The Natural," *Vogue*, September 2007, http://www.style.com/vogue/feature/2007_Sept_Michelle_Obama.

19. Quoted in Rosalind Rossi, "The Woman Behind Obama," *Chicago Sun Times*, January 20, 2007, www.suntimes.com/news/metro/221458,cst-nws-mich21.article.

20. Quoted in Mundy, *Michelle*, pp. 43–44.

21. Quoted in Colbert, *Michelle Obama*, pp. 53–54.

22. Quoted in Mundy, *Michelle*, p. 55.

23. Quoted in Tom Leonard, "Michelle Obama's Prom Date Describes Their High School Romance," *Daily Telegraph* (London), March 6, 2009, www.telegraph.co.uk/news/worldnews/northamerica/usa/michelle-obama/4949507/michelle-obamas-prom-date-describes-their-high-school-romance.html.

Chapter 2: College and A Career

24. Quoted in Maria L. La Ganga, "It's All About Priorities for Michelle Obama," *Los Angeles Times*, August 22, 2007.

25. Quoted in Wolffe, "Barack's Rock," p. 29.

26. Quoted in Mundy, *Michelle*, p. 58.

27. Quoted in Wolffe, "Barack's Rock," p. 29.

28. Quoted in Sally Jacobs, "Learning to Be Michelle Obama: At Princeton, She Came to Terms with Being a Black Achiever in a White World," *Boston Globe*, June 15, 2008, www.boston.com/news/nation/articles/2008/06/15/learning_to_be_michelle_obama.

29. Quoted in Brian Feagans, "Georgian Recalls Rooming with Michelle Obama," *Atlanta Journal-Constitution*, April 13, 2008, www.ajc.com/news/content/news/stories/2008/04/12/roommate_0413.html.

30. Quoted in Jacobs, "Learning to Be Michelle Obama."

31. Quoted in Andrew Herrmann, "How Princeton Shaped Michelle Obama's Views," *Chicago Sun-Times*, December 1, 2008, www .suntimes.com/news/politics/obama/1307497,cst-nws-mobama01.article.
32. Quoted in Chuck Klosterman, "Craig Robinson: America's First Coach," *Esquire*, February 2009, p. 54.
33. Quoted in Sarah Brown, "Obama '85 Masters Balancing Act," *Daily Princetonian*, December 7, 2005, www.dailyprincetonian. com/2005/12/07/14049.
34. Quoted in Karen Springen and Jonathan Darman, "Ground Support," *Newsweek*, January 29, 2007, p. 41.
35. Quoted in Brown, "Obama '85 Masters Balancing Act."
36. Michelle LaVaughn Robinson, "Princeton-Educated Blacks and the Black Community," senior thesis, Princeton University, 1985.
37. Quoted in Collins, "The Other Obama," p. 90.
38. Quoted in Herrmann, "How Princeton Shaped Michelle Obama's Views."
39. Robinson, "Princeton-Educated Blacks and the Black Community."
40. Quoted in Harvard Law School, "Michelle Obama's Commitment to Public Service Began at HLS," Harvard Law School, www.law .harvard.edu/news/michelle-obama-at-hls.html.
41. Quoted in Mundy, *Michelle*, p. 84.
42. Quoted in Wolffe, "Barack's Rock," p. 31.
43. Quoted in Liza Mundy, "When Michelle Met Barack," *Washington Post,* October 5, 2008.

Chapter 3: A New Career, Marriage, and Motherhood

44. Quoted in Rossi, "The Woman Behind Obama."
45. Quoted in David Mendell, *Obama: From Promise to Power*, New York: Amistad, 2007, pp. 93–94.
46. Barack Obama, *The Audacity of Hope: Thoughts on Reclaiming the American Dream*, New York: Crown, 2006, p. 330.
47. Quoted in Peter Slevin, "Her Heart's in the Race; Michelle Obama on the Campaign Trail and Her Life's Path," *Washington Post*, November 28, 2007.
48. Quoted in Mendell, *Obama*, p. 32.
49. Quoted in Christine G. Sabathia, "Meet Michelle Obama," *Los Angeles Sentinel*, October 25–31, 2007.

50. Quoted in Colbert, *Michelle Obama*, p. 93.
51. Quoted in Lauren R. Dorgan, "Falling in Love All over Again; Michelle Obama Gets a Warm Reception," *Concord Monitor* (New Hampshire), April 5, 2007.
52. Quoted in Peter Slevin, "Her Heart's in the Race."
53. Quoted in Andy Katz, "Brown Coach Robinson Coaching Brother-in-Law Obama, Too," ESPN, September 13, 2007, http://sports.espn.go.com/ncb/columns/story?columnist=katz_andy&id=3009012.
54. Quoted in Mundy, "When Michelle Met Barack."
55. Quoted in Johnson, "Natural," p. 777.
56. Quoted in Brown, "Obama '85 Masters Balancing Act."
57. Quoted in Wolffe, "Barack's Rock," p. 30.
58. Quoted in Rossi, "Woman Behind Obama."
59. Quoted in Cheryl Corley, "Michelle Obama: The Exec, Mom and Campaigner," National Public Radio, August 12, 2008, www.npr.org/templates/story/story.php?storyid=93535521.
60. Quoted in Perry Bacon Jr., "Forum Puts Obama's Heritage in Focus," *Washington Post*, August 7, 2007, http://voices.washingtonpost.com/44/2007/08/07/obama_black_enough.html.
61. Quoted in Wolffe, "Barack's Rock," p. 29.
62. Quoted in Michael Powell and Jodi Kantor, "After Attacks, Michelle Obama Looks for a New Introduction," *New York Times*, June 18, 2008, www.nytimes.com/2008/06/18/us/politics/18michelle.html?_r=1&pagewanted=1.

Chapter 4: A Politician's Wife

63. Quoted in Westfall, "Michelle Obama: This Is Who I Am," p. 120.
64. Quoted in Mendell, *Obama*, p. 99.
65. Quoted in Jay Newton-Small, "Michelle Obama's Savvy Sacrifice," *Time*, August 25, 2008, p. 38.
66. Obama, *Audacity of Hope*, p. 339.
67. Quoted in Collins, "Other Obama," p. 92.
68. Quoted in Mundy, *Michelle*, p. 133.
69. Quoted in Westfall, "Michelle Obama: This Is Who I Am," p. 120.
70. Quoted in Anne E. Kornblut, "Michelle Obama's Career Timeout; For Now, Weight Shifts in Work-Family Tug of War," *Washington*

Post, May 11, 2007.

71. Quoted in Johnson, "Natural," p. 776.
72. Obama, *Audacity of Hope*, p. 341.
73. Quoted in Mendell, *Obama*, pp. 151–52.
74. Obama, *Audacity of Hope*, p. 5.
75. Quoted in Mary Massingale, "Michelle Obama Says Faith Guides Her Husband," *State Journal-Register* (Springfield, IL), October 16, 2005.
76. Quoted in Peter Slevin, "Her Heart's in the Race."
77. Quoted in Rossi, "Woman Behind Obama."
78. Quoted in Dori Meinert, "Obama Takes Capitol by Storm," *State Journal-Register* (Springfield, IL), January 5, 2005.
79. Quoted in Christopher Benson, "Barack and Michelle Obama Begin Their Storied Journey," *Savoy*, February 2005, p. 60.
80. Quoted in Mundy, *Michelle*, p. 9.

Chapter 5: On a Fast Track to the White House

81. Quoted in Jeff Zeleny, "Q&A with Michelle Obama," *Chicago Tribune*, December 24, 2005, www.chicagotribune.com/news/local/chi-051224obamamichelle,0,4172582.story.
82. Quoted in Zeleny, "Q&A with Michelle Obama."
83. Quoted in Evan Thomas, "How He Did It," *Newsweek*, January 21, 2008, p. 40.
84. Quoted in Gwen Ifill, "Beside Barack," *Essence*, September 2007, p. 202.
85. Quoted in Melinda Henneberger, "Michelle Obama Interview: Her Father's Daughter," *Reader's Digest*, October 2008, p. 179.
86. Quoted in *Post and Courier*, "Helping Obama Kick the Habit," *Post and Courier* (Charleston, SC), February 15, 2007.
87. Quoted in La Ganga, "It's All About Priorities for Michelle Obama."
88. Quoted in Shira Schoenberg, "Michelle Obama Emphasizes Family Life," *Concord Monitor* (New Hampshire), December 6, 2007.
89. Quoted in Sarah Baxter, "America Hails the Rise of a New JFK," *Sunday Times* (London), January 6, 2008.
90. Quoted in John McCormick, "For the Obama Campaign, the Closer Is in the Family," *Chicago Tribune*, December 16, 2007, http://archives.chicagotribune.com/2007/dec/17/news/chi-closer_17dec17.
91. Quoted in Elizabeth Lightfoot, *Michelle Obama: First Lady of Hope*,

Guilford, CT: Lyons Press, 2009, p. xxi.

92. Quoted in Collins, "Other Obama," p. 93.

93. Quoted in Nancy Gibbs and Jay Newton-Small, "The War over Michelle," *Time*, June 12, 2008, p. 28.

94. Quoted in Collins, "Other Obama," p. 94.

95. Quoted in Anne E. Kornblut, "Michelle Obama's Career Timeout."

96. Quoted in John McCormick, "It's an Iowa Christmas for the Obamas," *Chicago Tribune*, December 16, 2007, http://archives .chicagotribune.com/2007/dec/17/news/chi-closer_ box_17dec17.

97. Quoted in Margaret Talev, "Obama Looks to His Wife to Build Him Up—and Knock Him Down," *Knight Ridder/Tribune News Service*, July 6, 2007.

98. Quoted in Ifill, "Beside Barack," p. 203.

99. Quoted in Scott Helman, "Michelle Obama Revels in Family Role," *Boston Globe*, October 28, 2007.

100. Michelle Obama, interview by Katie Couric, *CBS Evening News*, February 15, 2008, www.cbsnews.com/stories/2008/02/15 /eveningnews/main3838886.shtml.

101. Quoted in Abdon M. Pallasch, "Michelle Obama Celebrates Chicago Roots," *Chicago Sun-Times*, August 26, 2008, www .suntimes.com/news/politics/obama/1126753,cst-nws-dem26 .article.

102. Quoted in Abigail Pesta, "Michelle Obama Keeps It Real," *Marie Claire*, November 2008, p. 86.

103. Quoted in Scott Helman, "'Holding Down the Obama Family Fort," *Boston Globe*, March 30, 2008, www.boston.com/news /nation/articles/2008/03/30/holding_down_the_obama_ family_fort/.

Chapter 6: Life as the First Lady

104. Quoted in Manuel Roig-Franzia, "'At Last,' Obamas Dance at End of the Day/President and First Lady Attend 10 Celebrations," *Houston Chronicle*, January 21, 2009.

105. Quoted in *People*, "Magic Moments," *People*, February 2, 2009, p. 59.

106. Quoted in Liz Jones, "Michelle, a Simple Ray of Sunshine," *Daily Mail* (London), January 21, 2009.

107. Quoted in Richard Weir, "Inauguration 2009: Chic Prez, Wife

Usher in Era of 'Obamalot,'" *Boston Herald*, January 22, 2009.

108. Quoted in Julie Hinds, "Why Sleeveless? Because Michelle Obama Can," *Detroit Free Press*, March 2, 2009.

109. Quoted in Weir, "Inauguration 2009," p. 6.

110. Quoted in Pesta, "Michelle Obama Keeps It Real," p. 86.

111. Quoted in Andre Leon Talley, "Leading Lady: From Envisioning a More Inclusive White House to Embracing Fearless Fashion, Michelle Obama Is Poised To Become the Most Transformative First Lady in History," *Vogue*, March 2009, p. 504.

112. Quoted in Philip Sherwell, "Michelle Obama Persuades First Granny To Join New White House Team," *Daily Telegraph* (London), November 8, 2008, www.telegraph.co.uk/news/3407525/michelle-obama-persuades-first-granny-to-join-new-white-house-team.html.

113. Quoted in Sandra Sobieraj, "Michelle Obama 'We're Home,'" *People*, February 9, 2009.

114. Quoted in Oprah Winfrey, "Oprah Talks to Michelle Obama," *O the Oprah Magazine*, April 2009, p. 143.

115. Quoted in Richard Leiby, "First Lady's Job? Slowly, It's Hers to Define," *Washington Post*, February 20, 2009.

116. Quoted in DeNeen L. Brown, "At the State Department, Sisterhood," *Washington Post*, March 11, 2009, http://voices.washingtonpost.com/44/2009/03/11/at_the_state_department_sister.html?hpid=news-col-blog.

117. Quoted in Josh Freedom du Lac, "At White House Show, Truly a Night of Wonder!" *Washington Post*, February 26, 2009.

118. Quoted in Christi Parsons, "Michelle Obama's First Job: First Mom," *Chicago Tribune*, February 24, 2009, www.chicagotribune.com/news/chi-michelle-obama-web-only-feb24,0,2703324.story.

119. Quoted in *Milwaukee Journal Sentinel*, "Military Families Need Help, First Lady Says," *Milwaukee Journal Sentinel*, March 14, 2009.

120. Quoted in Tim Reid, "Glamour, Grit and Homespun Charm: Mrs. Obama Gets Another Day Job," *Times* (London), May 12, 2007.

121. Quoted in Leiby, "First Lady's Job?"

122. Quoted in Sabathia, "Meet Michelle Obama."

1964

Michelle LaVaughn Robinson is born in Chicago on January 17, 1964.

1981

Graduates from Whitney M. Young Magnet High School.

1985

Graduates from Princeton University.

1988

Graduates from Harvard Law School.

1988

Goes to work for Sidley and Austin, a Chicago law firm.

1989

Begins dating Barack Obama.

1991

Fraser Robinson, Michelle's father, dies on March 6; in July she begins working as an assistant to Chicago mayor Richard Daley.

1992

Marries Barack Obama on October 18.

1993

Becomes executive director of Public Allies.

1996

Becomes associate dean of student services at the University of Chicago.

1998
Daughter Malia is born on July 4.

2001
Daughter Natasha (Sasha) is born on June 10.

2002
Becomes executive director for community affairs at University of Chicago Hospitals.

2004
Barack Obama delivers the keynote address in August at the Democratic National Convention; in November he wins a seat in the U.S. Senate.

2005
Is promoted to vice president for community and external affairs at University of Chicago Hospitals.

2007
Barack Obama announces he will seek the Democratic nomination for president on February 10.

2008
Barack Obama wins the Iowa caucus on January 3; Barack accepts the Democratic nomination for president on August 28; Barack defeats Republican senator John McCain for president on November 4.

2009
On January 20, Barack Obama is sworn in as the 44th president of the United States and Michelle Obama becomes the nation's First Lady.

For More Information

Books

David Bergen Brophy, *Michelle Obama: Meet the First Lady*. New York: Collins, 2009. This book is a juvenile nonfiction biography of Michelle Obama.

Michelle Obama, *Michelle Obama: In Her Own Words*. New York: PublicAffairs, 2009. This book has more than two hundred quotations by Obama on a variety of subjects that are arranged in categories.

Internet Sources

Chicago Tribune, "Michelle Obama," *Chicago Tribune.com*, www.chicagotribune.com/topic/politics/michelle-obama-PECLB005380.topic. This informative *Chicago Tribune* newspaper web site has stories, photographs, video, and links to other sites about Michelle Obama.

Organizing for America, "Meet Michelle," Organizing for America, www.barackobama.com/learn/meet_michelle.php.

Web Sites

Facebook (www.facebook.com/pages/Michelle-Obama/22092775577). Michelle Obama's Facebook page includes a brief biography, photos, videos, and links to articles. A Facebook account is required for access to detailed information.

Michelle Obama Watch (http://michelleobamawatch.com). This Web site offers current news media stories, photos, and videos about Michelle Obama.

Mrs. O (www.mrs-o.org). This Web site is dedicated to the fashion of Michelle Obama, including photos and commentary on her outfits.

The White House (www.whitehouse.gov). This Web site provides information about Michelle Obama and all former First Ladies. The site also offers information about President Obama and the people and policies of his administration, details about the White House and its history, and a comprehensive section about the U.S. government.

Index

Michael V. Uschan has written over seventy books, including *Life of an American Soldier in Iraq* for which he won the 2005 Council for Wisconsin Writers Juvenile Nonfiction Award. Uschan began his career as a writer and editor with United Press International, a wire service that provided stories to newspapers, radio, and television. Uschan considers writing history books a natural extension of the skills he developed in his many years as a journalist. He and his wife, Barbara, reside in the Milwaukee suburb of Franklin, Wisconsin.